KINDERGARTER SNAKES

*A*dvantage
BOOKS

POETRY TO HELP UNCOIL A TWISTED WORLD

L. Richard De Prisco

Kindergarter Snakes by L. Richard De Prisco
Copyright © 2011 by L. Richard De Prisco
All Rights Reserved.
ISBN13: 978-1-59755-202-8

Published by: ADVANTAGE BOOKS™
                www.advbookstore.com

Library of Congress Control Number: 2011923451

Cover and Interior Illustrations
by Paul N. Ehmann.

First Printing: March 2011
11 12 13 14 15 16 17   10 9 8 7 6 5 4 3 2 1
Printed in the United States of America

DEDICATION

Do all books need a dedication?
So be it; let this one have one too, then, if it must.
But don't look for it here.
Conspicuous as it may be,
if the reader does not discover it in the pages that follow,
then stating it plainly on this particular page won't help.

But then again, isn't that what poetry is for?
To communicate in more artful but less direct ways
what prose could do by more straightforward means.

Then let poetry have its proper say and do its proper work.
I won't steal its thunder – or gentle mist – in this spot.
But don't worry – you can't miss it.

FOREWORD

Can poetry recover? Perhaps you never knew it was languishing in literary ICU in the first place. But according to a *Newsweek* report ("The End of Verse," March 25, 2009) there has been a precipitous decline in the reading of poetry by American adults over a 16-year period. The National Endowment of the Arts, while tracking an actual increase in the number of adults reading fiction, found that the number of poetry readers was falling at alarming rates. More than one in six adults had read poetry in a year's time in 1992. By 2002 that ratio had fallen to just under one in eight. By 2008 it had plummeted to approximately one in twelve – a 50% attrition in a little over a decade-and-a-half!

What could possibly be going on here? Has the American adult reader lost interest in a dying art form? Did tastes change virtually overnight, or have the practitioners failed their audience in a massive meltdown? Surely the demand continues to flow in one form or another, since all of contemporary music requires a huge input of poetic lyricism to satisfy the never-slaked thirst of the consuming public for new hits of all genres. And certain styles, like rap and hip-hop, rely less on melody and more on the spoken word for their appeal than other styles have in the past. Look at it another way: if food industry analysts observe that consumption of, say, crab goes down while consumption of pollock *made to taste like crab* goes up, they would likely entertain only two main explanations: either the supply of real crab has diminished, forcing prices up while limiting availability, or the imitation of the real thing is deemed "close enough," so fewer people are bothering to go to the trouble of seeking that real thing.

For poetry to stand on its own as a sought-after and appreciated medium of expression, four essential pillars are required (*pace*, free-verse writers!): rhythm, rhyme, reason, and resonance – call them the four "R's." Catchy song melodies can save poetry from itself when consumers content themselves with a good tune or an engaging beat and give up on gleaning anything from the lyrics. But when a musically unattached poem is wanting in two or more of these four foundational supports, its imbibers are sent away still thirsty to drink from the other genres at hand: the novel, the biography, the historical work, the newspaper, the gossip sheet, the political tract, the travelogue, the atlas, various Internet sites, bumper stickers, billboards, posters, T-shirts, or – in the empty desperation of that impoverished soul lured to the extreme form of anti-poetry – pornography.

How do the four "R's" conspire to make poetry work its magic? They combine linguistic structure, sound association, mental connection, and emotional appeal to embed the message deeply into the heart. It's really that last one – emotional appeal – that is served by the first three, and it doesn't matter whether it's humor, anger, sorrow, love, or hope that's targeted; the reaction evoked is all the more profoundly felt when the first three cylinders are all firing powerfully and efficiently. The poem actually makes it appear as if both the very structure and movement of language were designed expressly for the purpose of serving the sole interests of *that* particular creation. Likewise, the vocabulary marshaled also seems preordained for *that* poem. Words, even syllables, appear to have been crafted for *that* one peculiar handiwork only, an illusion not so apparent with prose.

There is an inherent price to pay, therefore, in hewing to the structural laws that make this artifice possible: multiple-syllable words don't all have accents where you want them in a particular place; there is a limited pool of words that rhyme with the one you need to rhyme with; stanzas, once formally built, forbid you to ramble on when you'd like to; a refrain must serve all stanzas, or else be written all over each time, yet still echo the first; a story or narrative must be told completely and movingly with little developmental time.

But a creditable product is worth the price. Moreover, if on occasion it reaches that rarefied level of value to the reader or hearer so as to mark out an indelible life lesson, goal, or remembrance, it can be memorized easily, or at least excerpts can be committed to memory. This, then, becomes the trigger for releasing the entire cargo of information and feeling that word strings effortlessly carry with them in a concise, unpacked form.

In a collection of poetry like this one, resonance occurs only according to the "vibes" of the reader or the particular "drummer's beat" that reader is marching to. The following list of poems is a motley one, loosely organized by subject or ambience/tone to appeal to a somewhat wide range of readers within a narrower spiritual context. Pick your device. One side note here: for this first volume, culled from a collection of poems that ranges even into deprecatory mode (yes, a Christian may go there – Psalmist David even staked out a place for the more searing *im*precatory verse, foreshadowing the harsh judgments of Christ Himself), only those of a somewhat tamer voice have been included here. Readers who might salivate for poems of a more "Dylanesque" variety will have to wait a while. Nevertheless, the sword of judgment is not altogether sheathed in the selections to come (see Chapter 6), but names aren't named and targets are wide and general.

It would be hard to create a large repository of poetic writings on Biblical themes without on occasion referencing to some degree the wrath of God against sin. Jesus was not just a "touchy-feely" preacher of soothing bromides. His words on numerous occasions were of such an incendiary nature that He got Himself crucified in the end. Perhaps at some point I'll incur some modern equivalent, but for now you may leave your heat shields in storage. At the outset, I'd more often have you chuckle than frown. Call it, if you will, spiritually-nutritionally fortified dessert to be eaten as an appetizer (in case you die soon).

It is my desire that you be enriched by each and every selection, and highly entertained in many cases. Let these poems abet your journey to a closer relationship with the High Poet of the songs of our lives.

NOTES
and
ACKNOWLEDGMENTS

The vast majority of the poems to follow are far better off without any introduction, and they know it. Where clarification is warranted beforehand a prefatory note is provided. However, a nod of gratitude is due to fellow writer, Vreni Schiess (author of the devotional book *Songs in the Night*), with whom I've enjoyed many hours of deep spiritual conversation – and maybe a similar number of hours of light, silly (but without coarse jesting!) banter – out of which have arisen many ideas for my poetry. I can't begin to capture all of them for a fair acknowledgement here, but I think these found at least a smidgen of their derivation in our many exchanges: "Called Every Name in the Book," "Outside the Box," "Nope, Just Can't, Sir," and "Crawling Butterflies." Memory fails me here in my effort to pinpoint others. So many more sprang from those many hours of sharing Scriptural insights, which is the marrow of deep Christian fellowship, but these do not now occur to me.

Charles Spurgeon's devotional writings would also deserve much credit for inspiration – Mrs. Schiess and I have spent a good deal of time "splurgin' on Spurgeon" to oil our discussions; too bad he isn't still around to thank in person. And I suppose I should tip my hat to Robert Service, the early twentieth century's "boreal bard." One would do well to aspire to the twinkle of the eye that glints from "The Cremation of Sam McGee."

Everything else is up to the reader to figure out. I've buried some hidden "winkers," as I call them, in scattered places. Some are quite obvious; others may be harder to mine; some I didn't intend at all, but discovered myself after the poem was finished and in the process of being edited. Those apparently are winkers to me from a higher source, and I think it not best not to clue you in in those cases as I believe they were meant for my own edification – it might ruin the effect for you if you were to learn they were "accidental."

Happy plumbing. May the springs you release provide for you a refreshment of the soul, heart, mind, and spirit. It may come as delight, conviction, wonder, edification, or even thought provocation. As long as you don't remain entirely unmoved I will be content with my effort. I hope to see you again in another volume, should this or any other publisher dare to show his face when I come knocking again.

Table of Contents

FOREWORD 4

NOTES AND ACKNOWLEDGMENTS...............................7

CHAPTER 1: THE CRUX OF THE MATTER 13
   Between the Lines.. 15
   Cross-Eyed Yes but Twenty-Twenty 17
   It's Out of My Hands... 19
   Bought the Farm 21
   Palm Springs 23

CHAPTER 2: HOW CAN YOU NOT LOVE THIS SAVIOR? 25
   Undying Love's Own Dying Lover 27
   Never Wasn't Soon Enough................................... 29
   Too Much More of You 31
   Applecartwheels 33

CHAPTER 3: PERSPECTACLES 35
   Hindsight Early on Foreseen.................................. 37
   As Much Eternity as Time Permits........................... 39
   Syndromicity.. 41
   Just Outside the Universe 43
   Scenic Underwear 45
   Homesick for a Place I've Never Seen...................... 47

CHAPTER 4: PILGRIMS' EGRESS................................ 49
   He's Better Off Without Ur.................................... 51
   If the Sky's the Limit 53
   Holiday from Heresies.. 55
   One Thing Left They Cannot Do 57
   Jerusalem Will Wait 59

CHAPTER 5: TIMES OF THE SIGNS 61
  Under the Rainbow 63
  Disappointment Book 65
  Killing Time 67
  Zodiac for Second Birth 69

CHAPTER 6: GET 'EM BEFORE THEY'RE HOT 71
  Abyssal Warming 73
  Should've Seen it Coming Down 75
  Primer for the Proper 79
  Postcard from the Netherlands 81
  Give It One More Shot 83
  Amen to That 85

CHAPTER 7: WATCH OUT FOR THE MINDFIELDS 87
  Youtuberculosis 89
  That's Just Not My Gift 91
  Wags that Dog Your Tail 93
  Then Be That Way 95
  Where Crazies Rule the Roost 97

CHAPTER 8: FRAYED SO 99
  Wolves' Clothing 101
  If You Can? 103
  One Sky's Falling at a Time 105
  Crawling Butterflies 107
  Acrophobic, Falling 109

CHAPTER 9: ROUGH AND STUMBLE 111
  Male Pattern Boldness 113
  Nope, Just Can't, Sir 115
  Mighty Servant Girl 117
  Warriors in Therapy 119
  Leave the Old Man There to Rot 121

CHAPTER 10: MAKER'S PREROGATIVE 123
  He Thought, Therefore I Am 125
  Who's to Blame? 127
  Called Every Name in the Book 129
  Velvet Ultimatum 131

CHAPTER 11: WINNING THE APPEAL PROCESS......................133
  Genius with Three Wishes.................................135
  Wisdom for Dummies.....................................137
  Lady of the Golden Streets..............................139
  Confessions of a Holy Man 141
  Soft Apocalypse..143
  Carpe Deum 145

CHAPTER 12: THE FIX IS IN 147
  Broken Dishes...149
  Healing Lame Excuses 151
  Levi's Genes...153
  Orthodox Orthotics.....................................155
  Like CPR for Corpses 157

CHAPTER 13: FUN-TRICK PONIES 159
  X-Word Puzzle...161
  Eight Lives Down 163
  Well, I Never ... !......................................165
  Nine in Ten Agree......................................167
  Unsalty Salt 169
  Poetic Mercy..171

CHAPTER 14: IT'S REALLY ALL ABOUT HIM 173
  The Lion's Share 175
  For the God Who has Everything.........................177
  Satellites Revolving Credit 179
  At Least He's in a Better Place 181

CHAPTER 15: REFLECTIONS AND REFRACTIONS 183
  Time Once Was 185
  Face Prints..187
  Evil Ever Gently Comes.................................189
  Rough the Winds.......................................191
  Turned to Snow..193

CHAPTER 16: AFTER AFFECTS (... ALL) 195
  Jordan Rising 197
  Outside the Box..199
  Tomorrow's Just the History You Haven't Seen..................201

Overtake the Undertaker 203
Kindergarter Snakes 205

ALPHABETICAL INDEX OF POEMS 209

CHRONOLOGICAL INDEX OF SCRIPTURAL REFERENCES 213

Chapter 1

The Crux of the Matter

Between the Lines
Cross-Eyed Yes but Twenty-Twenty
It's Out of My Hands
Bought the Farm
Palm Springs

L. Richard De Prisco

BETWEEN THE LINES

It's all right there in black and white
And read all over by the saints
But have I plumbed for deeper light
Unwritten in the portrait paints?

His nerves had endings by the score
And each were frayed beyond the pale
With unremitting pain that tore
The fabric of that human vale

But was this not the least extent
Of anguish in that shredded tent?

I've learned to read between the lines
Of scarlet trails that streaked His face
Such love with mercy there combines
To burn a vision of that trace
I've learned to read between the lines
That tracked His back with glistening gaps
Compassion there made no repines
I travel by those well-worn maps

Raw wounds felt in extremis throb
Yet hurts inside are more extreme
Just thinking physics I would rob
My Savior of that ache supreme

But was this not the least extent
Of anguish in that shredded tent?

I've learned to read between the lines

Of scarlet trails that streaked His face
Such love with mercy there combines
To burn a vision of that trace
I've learned to read between the lines
That tracked His back with glistening gaps
Compassion there made no repines
I travel by those well-worn maps

It's not the flesh that stung the most
A tortured soul gave up the ghost

His grief was not for shrieking sores
Where paroxysm there confines
The stripes of pain in bloody scores
I've learned to read between those lines

For further reflection:
Psa 22:14, 55:4, 89:32; Isa 53:4; Heb 2:9-10

CROSS-EYED YES BUT TWENTY-TWENTY

A double vision's taken hold
To make my twenty twenty-twenty
Views are truly manifold
To make a bad few good and plenty
Second looks won't bring a scourge
The mind's eye makes the twain converge

Aligning dual points of locus
Causes pix to come in focus

Each retina some light absorbs
Superior: two lines of sight
Unparalleled! – these angled orbs
When right looks left and left looks right
I see each side and both I stress
The God and Man parts never smear
I'll stick with being cross-eyed, yes,
But twenty-twenty makes it clear

For twenty days He trod the sand
No quick-and-dirty day-hike sortie
Still the Devil made Him stand
As twenty coupled into forty
Veering not from gruesome fate
His cross-eyed gazes kept Him straight

Aligning dual points of locus
Causes pix to come in focus

Each retina some light absorbs
Superior: two lines of sight

Unparalleled! – these angled orbs
When right looks left and left looks right
I see each side and both I stress
The God and Man parts never smear
I'll stick with being cross-eyed, yes,
But twenty-twenty makes it clear

Monocular will never do
To get a deeper death perception
Aiming pairs will make it true
The cross involved prevents deception

So eye the cross, that sharpest sign
Whose doctrine here is worth the bother
Jesus, human and divine
The splittin' image of His Father

For further reflection:
Matt 4:1-2, 5, 16:21, 26:64; John 10:30, 12:27, 14:8-10, 20:28;
Eph 2:13-16

IT'S OUT OF MY HANDS

They sing of the world, yes, He's got the whole thing
He holds all its lands
But says of provisions I'm praying He'll bring
"It's out of My hands"

I'm told He faced death so He knows all my grief
And He understands
But says when I beg for some soothing relief
"It's out of My hands"

I'll never slip through like the finest of sands
I'm still in His hands

The thought that He'll fumble just grips me with fear
It's grasping my soul
He grabs my attention and makes it so clear
He's still in control

They're bent on destruction and utter this cry
They'll burn us like brands
I seek for deliverance and get this reply
"It's out of My hands"

It's me whom I'm hoping His love will ensconce
Is that where He stands?
I crave His salvation and learn His response
"It's out of My hands"

I'll never slip through like the finest of sands
I'm still in His hands

The thought that He'll fumble just grips me with fear
It's grasping my soul
He grabs my attention and makes it so clear
He's still in control

Isaiah gives comfort and so do the Psalms
I'm etched in His palms

He tells me to keep all His wounds well in mind
Those dark reddish bands
And when I look deep I may "bloody well" find
It's out of His hands

For further reflection:
Psa 22:16; Isa 49:16; Mark 6:2; Luke 24:50; John 10:28-29, 13:3, 20:25-
28; Rom 10:21

BOUGHT THE FARM

A parable of sower's seeds
Recounted types (the total's four)
Another mentioned vineyard deeds
Whose owner renters did deplore
And then some aggie took on guys
Just loitering in labor squads
One landed gent did not despise
A Moab widow gleaning pods

Since they produce what's edible
They're fodder for descriptive spots
Their stories all are credible
So, yeah, I'll buy those harvest plots
The Teller's silo's filled with tales
Our "Kernel," dying, took the harm
He'll see some yields of bigger bales
That Scion sent, who bought the farm

Some strategies were not so keen
There's one who wanted barns too big
A prodigal walked off the scene
He hungered like a grunting pig
But one smart man invested well
The ending's got a little charm
He learned a secret not to tell
For treasure hid he bought the farm

Since they produce what's edible
They're fodder for descriptive spots
Their stories all are credible
So, yeah, I'll buy those harvest plots

The Teller's silo's filled with tales
Our "Kernel," dying, took the harm
He'll see some yields of bigger bales
That Scion sent, who bought the farm

The tilling comes from all His pains
He plants His rows without a plow
His furrows bring abundant grains
He'll have no need of furrowed brow

That Reaper isn't really grim
Bestowing fruits and veggies brought
I'm eating from the hand of Him
Who'll take me to the farm He bought

For further reflection:
Ruth 2:5-9; Isa 53:11-12; Matt 13:44, 20:1-16, 21:33-43; Mark 4:3-20;
Luke 12:16-21, 15:11-32; John 12:24

PALM SPRINGS

There's been a drought, the stream's dried out
A desiccated … vast land
We're parched as dust, a shriveled crust
This surely is our … last stand

No water here, the sun will sear
The cracks that split our … dry skin
Through arid waste we'll end posthaste
In graves that each one … fries in

But You have given … palm springs
And shown us what that … balm brings
Oasis in the sands
The river stays at … flood tide
A current where the … blood cried
We saw it from Your hands

A desert moan, a gasping groan
Our voice reduced to … last breath
The vultures wait, anticipate
The onset of our … fast death

Relentless heat, our burning feet
Bode terror of a … pyre fate
Escape cut off, an empty trough
Dooms each of us to … dire strait

But You have given … palm springs
And shown us what that … balm brings
Oasis in the sands
The river stays at … flood tide

A current where the … blood cried
We saw it from Your hands

A fountain hums, hydration comes
With moisture for a … thirst quench
We're pouring thanks, and filling tanks
Revived by just that … first drench

From brimming moats, we wet our throats
Our troubled voice made … calm sings
No more to creep, in joy we leap
From handstands launching … palm springs

For further reflection:
Psa 105:41; Isa 43:20, 49:16; John 4:13-14, 7:38, 20:25

Chapter 2

How Can You Not Love This Savior?

Undying Love's Own Dying Lover
Never Wasn't Soon Enough
Too Much More of You
Applecartwheels

L. Richard De Prisco

UNDYING LOVE'S OWN DYING LOVER

That "until death" part had not entered
Love and Lover always one
Relationship had ever centered
On eternal living Son
A kind of barrenness kept lasting
Through their union always true
They shared a meal that felt like fasting
'Til the fruitful time was due

Lamenting like a mournful plover
Love released her Beau but then
He let her weeping spirit hover
In the tomb that was His den
Their passion going undercover
As He fell to raise up men
Undying Love's own dying Lover
Forced to leave to come again

She longed for children in their mansion
Quietness so hard to bear
All rooms were crafted for expansion
Once He brought their offspring there
She would not bear His lone departure
Gone to carry back her brood
He bared His breast to poaching archer
Made as Yoke to be their food

Lamenting like a mournful plover
Love released her Beau but then
He let her weeping spirit hover
In the tomb that was His den

Their passion going undercover
As He fell to raise up men
Undying Love's own dying Lover
Forced to leave to come again

No split occurred and she'd discover
There had been no jilting then ....

In view together now forever
With their progeny at hand
The death blow failed to make them sever
Ties that bind them in their land
Affection wasn't unrequited
Everlasting single heart
Fair Love and Lover still united
Never more to *seem* apart

For further reflection:
Matt 11:29-30; John 6:48-51, 17:24-26, 1 Cor 13:5, 7-8; 2 Cor 8:9;
1 John 4:8, 16

NEVER WASN'T SOON ENOUGH

Long peering out from this gazebo swing
And waiting for the lovely sound of footfalls to approach
But I could not make out a single thing
Save distant hints of fallen feet where shadows now encroach
Four thousand times I stood … but no
You wanted not to come … but go
I couldn't wait another year to see you fail to show

How could I make you understand?
Unless I left this hallowed land
And ran out there to clasp you empty hand to empty hand

The time I made could stretch on out and run to endless days
My patience had no boundaries but every heartstring frays
When shafts of love are showered out but bring back no reply
I knew you couldn't try … I knew that I would die
If what it took was all I had to give in total sum
I ached with every cold rebuff
Prepared to linger here forever while you'd never come
But never wasn't soon enough

That siren song was one you'd often heard
It lured you on as you refused My every soft appeal
Though danger signs to you had not occurred
That voice you did not recognize was masked to hide what's real
Like someone you could trust … but who?
As if for no one else … but you
I couldn't wait to make a move or you'd have followed through

How could I make you understand?
Unless I left this hallowed land

And ran out there to clasp you empty hand to empty hand

The time I made could stretch on out and run to endless days
My patience had no boundaries but every heartstring frays
When shafts of love are showered out but bring back no reply
I knew you couldn't try ... I knew that I would die
If what it took was all I had to give in total sum
I ached with every cold rebuff
Prepared to linger here forever while you'd never come
But never wasn't soon enough

The time we'll have together here will never have an end
Our hearts will sing in unison, you've found your closest Friend
My streams of love are now requited by a willing soul
I know you've lost the hole ... I know I took the role
That you could never take upon yourself from where you stood
But soon that molting shell will slough
While "never" always leaves its love where "always" never would
Forever will be long enough

For further reflection:
John 10:3-5, 15:16; Rom 5:6, 9:22-23; 2 Cor 8:9; Gal 4:4; Phil 2:7

TOO MUCH MORE OF YOU

With hands and feet and ears and eyes
You're represented as a Son
But could mere pairs of each comprise
A God who's got a world to run?
To manage all the things You've made
Each billion sons, each billion suns
You must be more than what's displayed
An ounce disclosed but not the tons

Two extremes are tucked away
Or else we'd not connect
Contrast hearkens night and day
Much more than I suspect
Deepest parts You keep concealed
Now screened so I can't see
Too much more of You revealed
Or too much more of me

I thought I knew me in and out
But rarely glimpse the faintest part
Of all corruption, vice, and doubt
The wickedness that fills my heart
I guess I just can't handle all
The rot that permeates my soul
I think I'm thankful, leaking gall
Whose pictures sparingly You dole

Two extremes are tucked away
Or else we'd not connect
Contrast hearkens night and day
Much more than I suspect

Deepest parts You keep concealed
Now screened so I can't see
Too much more of You revealed
Or too much more of me

You sparsely parcel holy views
Of what men see of You
And trickle out traumatic news
Of all the sins You slew

Content that You breast both our cards
I'd venture humbly for a peek
Of truths so harsh they're kept by guards
So You play hide and I'll go seek

For further reflection:
Psa 139:17-18; Isa 55:8-9; Jer 17:9; Dan 2:30; John 9:40-41;
Rom 11:33-34; 1 Cor 14:25

APPLECARTWHEELS

Just had to be some other fruit
If so I think I'm filing suit
Maligned in Eden without proof
Yet orchard yields still hit the roof
The daily ones keep docs away
While pies and moms are tight to stay
But as I'm gorging sauce and tarts
I'm now upsetting apple carts

I have no truck with such a crop
Just fixing wagons while I shop

I'd love to polish status quo
But staid things stayed, now have to go
I'm produce picked right from His eye
Old transport means no more apply
These spokes have spoken far too long
With hubs released I can't go wrong
Exuberance has peaked, and how
I'm launching applecartwheels now

With joy like this I'd best not trudge
This mechanism needs a nudge
I see the merchants gasp and gulp
As they envision smashing pulp
But feeling giddy to the core
I cannot trundle anymore
These arms and legs have got to whirl
This wooden vessel's gonna hurl

I have no truck with such a crop

Just fixing wagons while I shop

I'd love to polish status quo
But staid things stayed, now have to go
I'm produce picked right from His eye
Old transport means no more apply
These spokes have spoken far too long
With hubs released I can't go wrong
Exuberance has peaked, and how
I'm launching applecartwheels now

Gymnastics always gives them fits
But I'm no longer in the pits

His sweet delights now make me spin
In ecstasy I'll shed my skin

For further reflection:
1 Chron 15:25-29; Psa 17:8; Song 2:3; Mark 2:22; Acts 3:8; 1 Pet 1:8

Chapter 3

Perspectacles

Hindsight Early on Foreseen
As Much Eternity as Time Permits
Syndromicity
Just Outside the Universe
Scenic Underwear
Homesick for a Place I've Never Seen

L. Richard De Prisco

HINDSIGHT EARLY ON FORESEEN

This running headlong onward looking back
Means not ahead for long but in the pack
And apt to trip on small protruding rocks
Delaying progress that the stumbling blocks

To stop and turn around might speed the pace
And watching me look back upon the race
That future face has many tales to tell
If in advance I'd study where I fell

So hard to see this me from where I stand
Comparing pending outcomes with the planned
And Monday quarterbacks too well predict
The Sunday upsets clairvoyants inflict
The me to come has eyes with much to speak
Of sure advice divulging what I seek
There is no vision ever quite so keen
As perfect hindsight early on foreseen

That older wiser me I glimpse beyond
Could help me in a time-abridging bond
His deep regrets I'd sorely like to know
Perhaps against a few I'd strike a blow

And what he's learned may not be hard to gauge
We both can read the same eternal page
It's just that he's more often seen it proved
I've seen my share but failed to see me moved

So hard to see this me from where I stand
Comparing pending outcomes with the planned

And Monday quarterbacks too well predict
The Sunday upsets clairvoyants inflict
The me to come has eyes with much to speak
Of sure advice divulging what I seek
There is no vision ever quite so keen
As perfect hindsight early on foreseen

So peering forward is the path to take
Distractions here are leaving in their wake
Provincial fears that bully and harass
Suggesting things that never come to pass

He's lost his faith but doesn't need it there
But begs me now to gaze and be aware
Those backward glancing eyes reveal to me
His hindsight's just the thing I should foresee

For further reflection:
Matt 16:2-3, 24:42-44, 25:13; Luke 12:54-56, 21:34-36; 1 Thes 5:1-8

AS MUCH ETERNITY AS TIME PERMITS

The sun that's watched just never sets
Except when you could wish it wouldn't ever cool its jets
Relief appears as altered states
When pain that throbs keeps coming back each time that it abates

What's loved and hated ebbs and flows
What good's the good if every time you find it comes and goes?

To grasp for endless now's insane
There's all forever to enjoy the bliss that will not wane
Don't lust for temporary bits
You're granted just as much eternity as time permits

What troubled souls will learn belief
If you won't ever bother being bothered by their grief?
If you'll be thankful for your hurts
Don't be surprised if you're surprised by timelessness in spurts

What's loved and hated ebbs and flows
What good's the good if every time you find it comes and goes?

To grasp for endless now's insane
There's all forever to enjoy the bliss that will not wane
Don't lust for temporary bits
You're granted just as much eternity as time permits

Redeem the time that drags (it's short)
You won't regret your sacrifice when reaching "last resort"

Don't rue the day that sorrows fill
Or clench the day when all you feel's the passing cloud-nine thrill

Unclouded by these fleeting things
You'll find eternity will come in time to end these swings

For further reflection:
Psa 103:15; Eccl 12:1; Matt 6:19-20; 1 Cor 4:16-5:4; Jas 4:14

SYNDROMICITY

The coffee just would not agree
Thus indigestion's grounds
For juiced up homicidal spree
So guilt is out of bounds

With hormones shooting off the scale
The words were not my own
Excuses should suffice for bail
When inhibition's blown

My sleep was clearly apneated
Judgment fled, I'm just a pawn
It's not a problem I created
Just not blessed with moral brawn
It's all the fault of my conditions
Robot in complicity
Should mitigate all harsh renditions
Blame the syndromicity

Short tempers now are all the rage
It weaponized my van
Bad chemicals had set the stage
Not me, I'm just a man

It's just a lapse
I missed my naps
No logs got sawed
My brain is flawed
Go finger drugs
Not rapist thugs
It's alcohol

That robbed the mall
You call it sin? I got to choose?
To err is human, what's to lose?
Responsibility's bad news
I'd rather sing some syndrome blues

My sleep was clearly apneated
Judgment fled, I'm just a pawn
It's not a problem I created
Just not blessed with moral brawn
It's all the fault of my conditions
Robot in complicity
Should mitigate all harsh renditions
Blame the syndromicity

It's some deficiency
Like inefficiency
I'm not omniscient, see?
No specificity
In all simplicity
It's syndromicity

For further reflection:
Isa 5:20-21; Luke 16:15; 2 Cor 10:12

JUST OUTSIDE THE UNIVERSE

That comrade peered from outer space
And came back with his full report
He couldn't find that blessed face
Unsettling was his settled snort
That few could make a swift retort

So how far out is far enough
To clear the air and call his bluff?

That land's not far beyond our hopes
But light years past the farthest curse
It can't be viewed through telescopes
You'll see it when they call the hearse
It's just outside the universe

The jilted lover dropped his gun
He'd dropped his competition cold
He hated what his hate had done
And in that rage his soul was sold
Some bars will stay when he's paroled

So how far out can guilt be sent
When all appeals on earth are spent?

That land's not far beyond our hopes
But light years past the farthest curse
It can't be viewed through telescopes
You'll see it when they call the hearse
It's just outside the universe

New wonder drugs some lives prolong

They seem robust but then decline
No miracles can keep them strong
They still end up all wrapped in pine
Recourse is not in earth's design

So how far out is paradise
Where fear of death can't be a vice?

That land's not far beyond our hopes
But light years past the farthest curse
It can't be viewed through telescopes
You'll see it when they call the hearse
It's just outside the universe

A space ship cannot get you there
So put it back in full reverse
A Navigator knows just where
You'll safely make the full traverse
It's just outside the universe

For further reflection:
2 Chron 6:18; Psa 103:12; 1 Tim 6:16; Rev 20:11, 21:1

SCENIC UNDERWEAR

That boxer hasn't fought too hard
To keep his belt above his hips
Was he tattooed or is he scarred?
We find out more each time it slips
A wonder it's allowed to show
Elastic bands see light of day
From accidents the surgeons know
If it's still light or seen its day

The cut revealing glory bright
Is not tucked in, kept out of sight

It's thick like robes and covers all
But never needs a scrubbing board
No strings attached to let it fall
The hidden vitals snugly stored
It's modeled in old walks of fame
That spotless laundry's made to air
So natty dressers feel no shame
In sporting scenic underwear

The better brand is made for looks
But not the kind that clings to skin
Its threads are found in sacred books
And truly meant for wear within
It's always white and never fades
And loved a bunch though smooth and clean
Its owners don it in parades
Designed with fabric to be seen

The cut revealing glory bright

Is not tucked in, kept out of sight

It's thick like robes and covers all
But never needs a scrubbing board
No strings attached to let it fall
The hidden vitals snugly stored
It's modeled in old walks of fame
That spotless laundry's made to air
So natty dressers feel no shame
In sporting scenic underwear

It's made to fit all sorts of souls
And moths will leave no tell-tail holes

On Judgment Day the finely clad
Take skivvies that won't leave them bare
So wear them "out" 'til all have had
A tour of scenic underwear

For further reflection:
Exo 20:26, 28:42-43; Lev 16:4; Isa 47:3; Matt 5:16; 2 Cor 4:16, 5:2-4;
Rev 3:18, 7:9-14

HOMESICK FOR A PLACE I'VE NEVER SEEN

It's déjà vu but not again
I'd never seen it way back then
And yet I know it like my hand
It isn't new (least, as in "brand-")
When I go back I'll reminisce
And recognize that edifice
That memory will never die
As God's my witness, nor will I

The taste I have has been acquired
Without one preview here required

Reminded by familiar shapes
I've tread those carpets, pulled those drapes
The mattress has my body's mold
Those marks of height are mine I'm told
A whiff brings back uncanny smell
Of garden fragrance known so well
I've got an inkling what's in store
A future time from days of yore
And now I find I'm homesick for … a place I've never seen before

My maiden voyage hasn't sailed
But former trips I have regaled
It's not the first time here on board
That harbor skyline strikes a chord
New songs I hear off starboard bow
I mouth the words, but don't know how
Accustomed to this textured wheel
Initial touch, recurring feel

The taste I have has been acquired
Without one preview here required

Reminded by familiar shapes
I've tread those carpets, pulled those drapes
The mattress has my body's mold
Those marks of height are mine I'm told
A whiff brings back uncanny smell
Of garden fragrance known so well
I've got an inkling what's in store
A future time from days of yore
And now I find I'm homesick for ... a place I've never seen before

Come, Lord, now and take the helm
Lest recognition overwhelm

My recall so complete for one
Who's never glimpsed the oft-seen Son

For further reflection:
John 14:21-23; 16:13-15, 20:29; Heb 11:13-16

Chapter 4

Pilgrims' Egress

He's Better Off Without Ur
If the Sky's the Limit
Holiday from Heresies
One Thing Left They Cannot Do
Jerusalem Will Wait

L. Richard De Prisco

HE'S BETTER OFF WITHOUT UR

There once his lofty stature could astound
With vital Ur-gent rank in Ur society
But splendor's vanished ever since he found
Ur majesty bereft of any piety

That settlement lies far behind him now
The settlement he signed with sweating brow
Might set Ur jaw and bring a stern Ur scow
But prove in time it's far the better vow

She beckons with Ur comfort zones
Bewilderment with things held dear
But wilderness will make no bones
He's better off without Ur here

The citificd appeal no longer feeds
The stylish and Ur-bane of his existence when
That naughty boy of bygone days recedes
He vainly kept that Ur-chin up so high back then

That settlement lies far behind him now
The settlement he signed with sweating brow
Might set Ur jaw and bring a stern Ur scow
But prove in time it's far the better vow

She beckons with Ur comfort zones
Bewilderment with things held dear
But wilderness will make no bones
He's better off without Ur here

Though once he had Ur eating from his hand
He bet Ur that he'd find a better land
He's bored Ur with a parting script unplanned
Her border lies outside the hills he's scanned

She bit Ur lips and uttered bitter pleas
He won't go back no matter what he sees
She'd bat Ur eyes and draw him with a wink
Or batter him with lies and closer slink
"Oh, honey, so well-bred, you must return,"
She beckons but Ur calls he'll only spurn
His bread and butter drips with honey clear
He knows he's better off without Ur here

For further reflection:
Gen 11:31; Neh 9:7; Heb 11:8-10, 14-16

IF THE SKY'S THE LIMIT

So long ago when we were squirts
The snow would often reach our hips
But now with shins it barely flirts
What caused accumulation dips?

I guess we had our sights too low
And things get smaller as we grow

Expanse of space won't let you trim it
If you're reaching for a star
That sea's too wide for you to swim it
Heaven's not conceded par
Yet lofty clouds can never dim it
If you set a higher bar
Remember if the sky's the limit
You're not going very far

Horizons keep on pushing back
And make the dawn extend its rays
When ceiling plaster starts to crack
Then light years crumble into days

I guess our earthly vision's small
And causes soaring dreams to stall

Expanse of space won't let you trim it
If you're reaching for a star
That sea's too wide for you to swim it
Heaven's not conceded par
Yet lofty clouds can never dim it
If you set a higher bar

L. Richard De Prisco

Remember if the sky's the limit
You're not going very far

Your firmament could be exalted
Way beyond this ether spread
And no trajectories are halted
When all boundaries have fled

Since God is boundless then to Him it
Doesn't matter where you are
When you discern the sky's no limit
He won't seem so very far

For further reflection:
Deut 10:14; 1 Kings 8:27; Acts 1:9-11; 2 Cor 12:2; Eph 4:10; Rev 11:12

HOLIDAY FROM HERESIES

Clanging forks and popping corks
Festivities have broken out but didn't they just lately end?
Cancelled shifts and giving gifts
As soon as this one's done another one's around the bend

Curious I hesitate
What's it now we celebrate?
Oh, this or that it matters not but hurry now and don't be late

Christmas made by polar dwarf
And Easter brought by lagomorph
They're basing all the pomp on circumstantial evidence
Bother not with history
It's far more fun as mystery
With sources shrouded holidays are viewed as heaven sense
Scrutinize with shuttered eyes
Reasons known by clerisy
What's the cause that brings applause?
Bound to be some heresy

Can I shake this need to fake?
Vacations of the mind are mindless means for getaway
Ritual habitual
Commemorating true events the better grounds to mark a day

Curious I hesitate
What's it now we celebrate?
Oh, this or that it matters not but hurry now and don't be late

Christmas made by polar dwarf
And Easter brought by lagomorph

They're basing all the pomp on circumstantial evidence
Bother not with history
It's far more fun as mystery
With sources shrouded holidays are viewed as heaven sense
Scrutinize with shuttered eyes
Reasons known by clerisy
What's the cause that brings applause?
Bound to be some heresy

Pack real light then book a flight
Escaping all obligatory sites along the way
Tourists snap and set their trap
But locals know the place to go to get above the fray

Radical sab-bad-ical
To trade these winds and sail away to find so rare a breeze
Hate a rite that isn't right?
Then bake a cake and take a break from all those Pharisees
On holiday from heresies

For further reflection:
Neh 8:10-12; Esther 9:17-22; 1 Cor 13:6; Phil 4:8; Rev 11:10-13

ONE THING LEFT THEY CANNOT DO

Shoved, I buckle to my knees
There in front of Damocles
Made to utter pretty please
Round one just a warm-up tease
Not their god I must appease
At their threats I merely sneeze

What they think they've won is Pyrrhic
So I'll write triumphant lyric ....

Life I hold is hostage fare
While it lasts they lay it bare
Cranking up each sore travail
Claiming conquest when I fail
Still they'll meet their Waterloo
One thing left they cannot do
Keep me past the day I'm due

Lots of things still up their sleeve
Dangle me from high-rise eave
Take my loved ones so I'll grieve
Make belief seem make-believe
Yet they can't stop my reprieve
Stripped of power when I leave

What they think they've won is Pyrrhic
So I'll write triumphant lyric ....

Life I hold is hostage fare
While it lasts they lay it bare
Cranking up each sore travail

Claiming conquest when I fail
Still they'll meet their Waterloo
One thing left they cannot do
Keep me past the day I'm due

Beat me; treat me … heal the wound
Bend me; mend me … get me tuned
Curse me; nurse me … when I've swooned
But that cycle has to quit
When my heart stops … so does it

They'll take shots while I'm alive
Someday though I won't revive
"Easter seals" won't let them through
That's one thing they cannot do

For further reflection:
Psa 118:6; Matt 10:28; Rom 8:35-39; 1 Cor 3:17; Heb 13:6; 1 John 4:4

JERUSALEM WILL WAIT

The beds are soft, with pillows fluffed
But can't compare with ones at home
With pleas for my return rebuffed
To kiss again familiar loam
I know it's better here than dead
But life's fair luster fades to bleak
Accommodating is my dread
That lovely mount is all I seek

And all things Babylonian
Remind me that it's not my place
This exile move's Draconian
Each shameful day revives disgrace
And yet I'm told to plant my vines
And cultivate the foreign tree
I'd just entreat Him for some signs
Jerusalem will wait for me

I can't go back, that land laid waste
Must first receive its Sabbath rest
He razed it in His wroth distaste
And must restore its fallen crest
I'm told I have a mission here
Though sore oppressed with garments rent
My captors' doom is edging near
Their renovation's why I'm sent

And all things Babylonian
Remind me that it's not my place
This exile move's Draconian
Each shameful day revives disgrace

And yet I'm told to plant my vines
And cultivate the foreign tree
I'd just entreat Him for some signs
Jerusalem will wait for me

She's grown in beauty in my mind
In every gemstone facet's shade
Those memories I oft rewind
But rue the tragic fall replayed

From heights sweet comforts are declared
In whiter raiment I'll reside
From walls rebuilt a splendor's bared
That constitutes a comely bride
I'll need not run, her courts to meet
Descending majesty I'll see
He'll cast that pearl to kosher feet
Jerusalem's hill gate for me

For further reflection:
2 Chron 36:11-21; Ezra 6:3-22; Jer 29:4-14, 31:1-9; Dan 9:16-19;
Zech 7:9-8:23; Rev 21:2-21

Chapter 5

Times of the Signs

Under the Rainbow
Disappointment Book
Killing Time
Zodiac for Second Birth

UNDER THE RAINBOW

It came upon a midday cloudy
Arc above an ark it rose
The promise of a dry-out process
Flooding peace to interpose

And somewhere far beneath those colors
Olive-bearing white bird flew
Propitiated wrath prefigured
Bursting "damns" that no one knew

High above it mansions sprawling
Wait for occupants to rise
Now upon a Star they're calling
One Who walks below the skies
Wishes answered while they're waiting
In the meantime dreams come true
Clouds begin evaporating
Underneath that rainbow hue

All troubles dissipating upward
As through chimney tops dispersed
Then answers fall like raindrop candies
While no heights need be traversed

So why oh why can't I just point out
Overarching spectral bands
And show lost earth-bound skyward gazers
Pots of gold down in their lands?

High above it mansions sprawling
Wait for occupants to rise

Now upon a Star they're calling
One Who walks below the skies
Wishes answered while they're waiting
In the meantime dreams come true
Clouds begin evaporating
Underneath that rainbow hue

For further reflection:
Gen 9:12-17; Matt 6:9-10; John 14:1-3, 13-14

DISAPPOINTMENT BOOK

I need to squeeze another in
This week just looks completely full
Next Tuesday's schedule's rather thin
But I don't have the strings to pull
This calendar I'd love to clear
So I could pencil in the type
That sends no tears to thin my beer
For better news I'm growing ripe

I've tried to lower expectations
So these meetings can be dropped
Or make some reinterpretations
Proving that the pain has stopped
I find this volume's not conducive
To the facts I'd love to cook
And so the let-downs so intrusive
Jam my disappointment book

The lesson that I've slowly learned
Is that some good news will emerge
Although I want all bridges burned
By faith I must resist the urge
When things don't go the way I'd like
There's something rosy in the mix
So when the disillusions strike
Rebounding comes when meaning clicks

I've tried to lower expectations
So these meetings can be dropped
Or make some reinterpretations
Proving that the pain has stopped

I find this volume's not conducive
To the facts I'd love to cook
And so the let-downs so intrusive
Jam my disappointment book

Agendas once were mostly Spartan
When I cancelled what deflates
Yet all encounters that dishearten
Are the keys for brighter gates

The things that test my hope still mount
I see them stacked each time I look
Their slots are more than I can count
They fill my disappointment book
I know when I review those sheets
Each date assignment's from my Boss
Since gains to come exceed defeats
I'll just look forward to each loss

For further reflection:
Job 7:2-4, 23:14-17; Psa 22:5; Eccl 3:1; Lam 1:15; Jonah 1:17, 4:6-8;
Rom 5:5, 9:33

KILLING TIME

I see it as a mercy hit
Bare life support was all that ever kept it here
But that's all right, there's more of it
And if supplies run low a stockpile's always near

I wouldn't call it "tempicide"
Like stepping on a bug would bring no guilty plea
Surviving time has never cried
And for the deed I'm facing no real penalty

It's so annoying when it drags
It just deserved to get the snuffing that it got
Its absence raises no red flags
Good riddance; now there's less to linger on and rot

And yet the dirty deed still nags
With every loss my spirit sags
I feel no liberation by this petty crime
Each death just makes the numbness build
I wonder now what else I've killed
I'm haunted while I'm killing time

I shiver in cold-blooded chill
The morgue is filling but I'm getting nowhere fast
The more that comes the more I spill
It's now become a race to see who's standing last

And yet the dirty deed still nags
With every loss my spirit sags
I feel no liberation by this petty crime
Each death just makes the numbness build

L. Richard De Prisco

I wonder now what else I've killed
I'm haunted while I'm killing time

A sign of some surprise attack?
When every parking meter's saying time's expired
Afraid these days to turn my back
And off my guard I'll be the one who gets retired

It's murder trying all these means
To rid my mind of ghastly scenes
There's got to be a better way that's more sublime
My watch has hands that labor on
And when that final second's gone
I'll have to keep appointment at His killing time

For further reflection:
Matt 24:42-51; Mark 13:20, 33-37; Eph 5:15-16; Col 4:5

ZODIAC FOR SECOND BIRTH

They're always asking what's my sign
I have no snappy come-back line
I'll read the paper for this news
I'm down on luck but look for clues
And in my horror, scope the page
For wise predictions from a sage
With months and days combining wrong
Ill fate will get me 'fore too long

The cross, the only sign I need
"Divining" all that's been decreed

From Zanesville out to Zanzibar
Our constellation has one Star
From Idyllwild to Isle of Wight
The future's really looking bright
From Paraguay to Palestine
We're studying a better sign
From Raleigh to the Rio Grande
We fall in that new "Leo" band

A seer-sucker's born each sec
All tea leaves in this fraud he'll check
This always leaves me Ouija-bored
And wanting solid truth restored
Prognosticating what's to pass
Will outperform all crystal glass
What's coming next has been disclosed
Since Scripture canon first was closed

The cross, the only sign I need

"Divining" all that's been decreed

From Key West up to Kodiak
We've got a brand-new Zodiac
From Paris right on down to Perth
There's Zodiac for second birth
From Flint and Fargo to Fort Worth
New Zodiac's for second birth
Now all believers 'round the earth
Seek Zodiac for second birth

For further reflection:
Matt 12:38-41, 16:1-3; 1 Cor 1:22-25; Gal 6:14; Phil 1:27-28;
Rev 5:5, 15:1

Chapter 6

Get 'Em Before They're Hot

Abyssal Warming
Should've Seen it Coming Down
Primer for the Proper
Postcard from the Netherlands
Give It One More Shot
Amen to That

L. Richard De Prisco

ABYSSAL WARMING

If Chicken Little's "bucking" trends
Whose end is near? It all depends
When Kermit croaks he terminates
His panel part in fate debates
Though frogs die boiling by degrees
Their death comes fast with sudden freeze
More ice is nice but either way
That climate model's not in play

It's global for the ones still here
Ignoble once they disappear

I'm warming up on other fronts
To weather far beyond this sphere
I'll cool my heels there, I'm no dunce
Abyssal warming's what I'd fear
God's thermostat's got dual sets
But knobs are placed way out of reach
It's better here to hedge your bets
Than find below that spa's no beach

Would greenhouse gas abate your breath?
If methane scares, lay off the meth
No carbon credits buy you time
Right now you've got the nicer clime
Can't hold this temp 'cuz it's got legs
Don't cook the goose that lays your eggs
I wouldn't waste my vote if I
Were next of kiln (please notify)

It's global for the ones still here

Ignoble once they disappear

I'm warming up on other fronts
To weather far beyond this sphere
I'll cool my heels there, I'm no dunce
Abyssal warming's what I'd fear
God's thermostat's got dual sets
But knobs are placed way out of reach
It's better here to hedge your bets
Than find below that spa's no beach

This all will melt with fervent heat
You'll need a cooler place to meet
Your glacial change must come about
Don't sweat this heat, stay cool, chill out

For further reflection:
Matt 25:41; Luke 16:22-25; 2 Pet 3:10-12; Rev 16:8-9

SHOULD'VE SEEN IT COMING DOWN

Eve and Adam didn't see a tree Root, tripped, and took the Fall
Cain just got himself dis-Abel-ed – *brother!* (Couldn't he recall?)
Lot's dear wife was quite a looker, but she wasn't worth her salt
Aaron's sis played handily her Snow White part down to a fault
Epic-watching king of Bezek: two thumbs up was his desire
Nadab and Abihu fumed, but: "pyre, pyre, pans on fire!"
Achan's buried metals turned to stones that turned and buried him
Amorites found hail's not merry when it's sized like Anakim

Sadly, oafish jesters taunt like fool Goliath, headless clown
Our own world is just like Noah's, where each sinner's doomed to drown
Weather service warnings posted couldn't save Gomorrah-town
Caveats were everywhere; they should have seen it coming down
Should've known they had it coming; should've seen it coming down
Coming down … to your town … just look up, it's coming down

Ehud gave that secret handshake; Eglon left some weight behind
Migraines pained Abimelech when woman trouble messed his mind
Jael found she had his number – Sisera's (she had him pegged)
Pharaoh's baker had a sore throat; so did Haman, though he begged
When from Esther his own fate he was so "Mordecai'd" to learn
Korah and his friends got dropped off but their ride had no return
Absalom just banked at branches but got stuck with higher points
Philistines made sport of Samson but he crashed their party joints

Sadly, oafish jesters taunt like fool Goliath, headless clown
Our own world is just like Noah's, where each sinner's doomed to drown
Weather service warnings posted couldn't save Gomorrah-town
Caveats were everywhere; they should have seen it coming down
Should've known they had it coming; should've seen it coming down
Coming down … to your town … just look up, it's coming down

Satraps thought that they had Daniel licked, but lions licked their chops
Jericho, all walled-off (not Astoria), had room-rate drops
Egypt sent collection agents drowning in a sea of red
Evening stroll cost David's kid his life (he should have stayed in bed)
Knock-kneed king Belshazzar stumbled when some cursive words were penned
"Cursive" words to David also did in "Shimmy" in the end
Captive Zedekiah looked unsightly in Chaldeans' eyes
Zacharias fathered "Johnny … lately" ("mute-'nts" tell no lies)

Sadly, oafish jesters taunt like fool Goliath, headless clown
Our own world is just like Noah's, where each sinner's doomed to drown
Weather service warnings posted couldn't save Gomorrah-town
Caveats were everywhere; they should have seen it coming down
Should've known they had it coming; should've seen it coming down
Coming down … to your town … just look up, it's coming down

Warm-hand Luke wrote lengthy chapters pointing to the Savior's plight
Judas gave back all the dough but warranties ran out that night
Yet this guarantees that someday when you see that fiendish beast
And false prophet smelling sulfur, just the dragon gets released
But his bail runs out in no time; then he joins the other two
As the floodgates fling wide open swallowing a wicked crew
While the ones in robes of white will see the whole thing going down
Safely placed on higher ground they'll all be kept from going down

Sadly, oafish jesters taunt like fool Goliath, headless clown
Our own world is just like Noah's, where each sinner's doomed to drown
Weather service warnings posted couldn't save Gomorrah-town
Caveats were everywhere; they should have seen it coming down
Should've known they had it coming; should've seen it coming down
Coming down … to your town … just look up, it's coming down

Just like Jonah with big scuba we don't really need to drown
Nineveh still got the message though the prophet wore a frown

Check the skies and feel the chill, observe the leaves all turning brown
Don't descend like Jack and Jill and, lacking water, forfeit crown

For further reflection:
Gen 3:6, 4:8-9, 7:17-23, 19:24-26, 40:20-22; Exo 14:5-9, 23-28;
Lev 10:1-2; Num 12:1-10, 16:31-33; Deut 2:10; Josh 6:1, 20, 7:20-26,
10:11; Judg 1:4-7, 3:15-22, 4:17-22, 9:52-54, 16:25-30; 1 Sam 17:43-51;
2 Sam 11:2-4, 13-18, 16:5-8, 18:9-15; 1 Kings 2:42-46; Esther 6:12, 7:6-
10; Jer 52:8-11; Dan 5:2-6, 25-30, 6:4-24; Jonah 1:17, 3:4-10, 4:1; Matt
16:1-4, 27:3-5; Mark 13:28-29; Luke 1:18-22, 59-63, 12:54-57, 22:1-
23:46; Rev 19:20, 20:1-4, 10-15, 22:14

L. Richard De Prisco

PRIMER FOR THE PROPER

Pinky ... just extended so
Earl Gray would give his high approval
Kinky ... if the furs are faux
But looking at abrupt removal

The debonair and nouveau riche
Run stiff soufflé to soupy quiche

By propping up their empty suit
The prim are fine and dandy
The fops are fey and just too cute
Disguising rank and randy
It's all about the polished self
The gauche will come a cropper
Best seller flying off the shelf
Is "Primer for the Proper"

Tailors ... keep the collars crisp
The coif is sharp and highly rigid
Hailers ... feint the faintest lisp
Their buss – say, "mwah!" – runs cool to frigid

The debonair and nouveau riche
Run stiff soufflé to soupy quiche

By propping up their empty suit
The prim are fine and dandy
The fops are fey and just too cute
Disguising rank and randy
It's all about the polished self
The gauche will come a cropper

Best seller flying off the shelf
Is "Primer for the Proper"

For candid shots they slip a tsk
Because façades reduce their risk
Of crimping sales still running brisk
But some are crying in their bisque

They're putting on the greatest show
Their act is quite a stopper
Impressing grandees in the know
These pampered prim and proper
Their self-deceit is bound to grow
They're looking for a topper
But soon that sham will have to go
Just throw it in the hopper

For further reflection:
Prov 11:22; Matt 23:25-28; John 7:24; 1 Tim 2:9-10; Jas 2:1-4, 5:1-5

POSTCARD FROM THE NETHERLANDS

(Note: the first four lines of the first stanza are in the voice of the postcard recipient; the remaining lines in this stanza and all others are in the voice of the postcard sender; the refrain is in the voice of the narrator.)

Oh, look, there's something here from Richie saying where he went
Across some sea where now he's stuck; his mood seems diffident
I'd heard he'd been "sent up" – some "river sticks" out in my mind
Let's read his "glowing" tale of "tripping," see what we can find ....
"I thought I'd booked a Holland line but 'crews' is what I'm on
No stewards seem to be around; I slave from dusk to dawn
This isn't what I'd call a treat although we all go Dutch
No gambling here but each must ante up for sins and such"

No matter who you deal with there they're in the underworld
All residents are "low-life" types, it's where they all get hurled
What happens there just stays right there and there is no reprieve
No need to check out from hotels since you can never leave
Don't think that all who journey on are in a better place
Communiqués might look real glossy but can't make the case
It all seems murky yet there's one thing really crystal clear
A postcard from this Netherlands is not a souvenir

"I've wandered through the streets today but haven't found The Hague
I'm telling you, this dump's a "dive," avoid it like the plague!
Those wooden shoes are not the kind you'd ever want to wear
They just combust too fast and burning feet are hard to bear
The summers here just go all year and scorching winds can singe
And every day's a bad-hair day; the soot would make you cringe
I try to lower thermostats – they're all pre-set for hikes
Some 'rotter' dams have holes but guards keep fingers in those dikes"

No matter who you deal with there they're in the underworld
All residents are "low-life" types, it's where they all get hurled
What happens there just stays right there and there is no reprieve
No need to check out from hotels since you can never leave
Don't think that all who journey on are in a better place
Communiqués might look real glossy but can't make the case
It all seems murky yet there's one thing really crystal clear
A postcard from this Netherlands is not a souvenir

"These windmills just keep fanning flames (I think that's all they're for!)
The Gouda melts outside your mouth (bare tongues would not endure)
The 'bakery' is where we dwell but not where people shop
Untended gardens wilt down here (but where's that TULIP crop?)
I recognized some beggar lounging out across the bay
He wouldn't spare a dime or even give the time of day
I asked him for a drop of water, but a great divide
Prevented any shuttle craft from giving him a ride"

No matter who you deal with there they're in the underworld
All residents are "low-life" types, it's where they all get hurled
What happens there just stays right there and there is no reprieve
No need to check out from hotels since you can never leave
Don't think that all who journey on are in a better place
Communiqués might look real glossy but can't make the case
It all seems murky yet there's one thing really crystal clear
A postcard from this Netherlands is not a souvenir

"I know your cherished 'Travelogue' warns tourists of this spot
Forget this 'destination' town though nightlife here is hot
Please tell my brothers, stay away! – this hole should be their dread
They act like Zombies so, you think, they'll heed the living dead?"

For further reflection:
Matt 25:41; Luke 16:19-31; John 8:23-24

GIVE IT ONE MORE SHOT

It's looking pretty scraggly there
I told Him that it's fine as is and none the worse for wear
He nearly yanked it by the root
I begged Him just to wait another year or so for fruit

He said it's only wasting ground
Then shook His head and grimly frowned
His patience wanes, it's wearing thin
He'll let me give it one more spin

As deadline looms it's very hectic
Got to try all plans eclectic
Conjure up a plot
This salvage job's my dialectic
Must not see Him apoplectic
Give it one more shot

I dig and water, raise the stakes
My efforts must succeed right now, no matter what it takes
The fertilizer sinks in quick
I'm in deep do-do if this work just doesn't do the trick

He said it's only wasting ground
Then shook His head and grimly frowned
His patience wanes, it's wearing thin
He'll let me give it one more spin

As deadline looms it's very hectic
Got to try all plans eclectic
Conjure up a plot
This salvage job's my dialectic

Must not see Him apoplectic
Give it one more shot

The pace I've set is furious, I've got no time to spare
He's sure to chop it down next time He comes and finds it bare

I cannot bear to think the thought that I might see some day
A bullet-riddled plot
With rifle raised He squints and then I wince to hear Him say
I'll give it one more shot

For further reflection:
Deut 29:22-28; Matt 3:10, 7:19, 21:19; Luke 13:6-9; Heb 6:7-8

AMEN TO THAT

Bring it, brother – make 'em weep! Shear those sheep; amen to that!
Bend that Bible – scream the Word! Just be heard; amen to that!
Preach till midnight – altar calls! Shake the walls; amen to that!
Open wallets – drop some green? Times are lean; let's have a chat

Politicians – give 'em heck! Wring their neck; amen to that!
Business moguls – dress 'em down! Scowl and frown; amen to that!
Wretched lechers – make 'em sweat! Let 'em fret; amen to that!
Be a witness – take a stand? Give a hand? We'll think on that

With you now in one accord
Just don't ever get our gourd
We're "amenable" to things
Where the message never stings
Tickled ears is what we like
Other cads should feel the spike
Only when the answer's pat
Will we say amen to that

Teen rebellion – kids these days! Cuff those strays; amen to that!
Drunks and druggies – ride 'em hard! Have 'em tarred; amen to that!
Thieves and bandits – don't set free! Toss the key; amen to that!
Be forgiving – fairly deal? Maybe we'll … get back on that

Hollywoodniks – skewer all! Mock their fall; amen to that!
Shabby dressers – clean their act! Use no tact; amen to that!
Wimps and sissies – buck 'em up! Scare 'em? Yup; amen to that!
Don't eat camels – clear out throat? Find no mote? We'll strain a gnat

With you now in one accord
Just don't ever get our gourd

We're "amenable" to things
Where the message never stings
Tickled ears is what we like
Other cads should feel the spike
Only when the answer's pat
Will we say amen to that

Only one sharp edge per sword
Keeps our ox from getting gored
When it's theirs the hatchet swings
Not on us indictment clings
Stick their heads upon the pike
Call on us no lightning strike
But if we should smell a rat
You won't hear amen to that

Hypocrites will soon fall flat
Since these judges never sat
Where God (seeing Hades' vat)
Points and says, "'Ey, men: to that!"

For further reflection:
Matt 23:13-33; Luke 6:41-42; 2 Tim 3:2-5, 4:3; Jas 1:22

Chapter 7

Watch Out for the Mindfields

Youtuberculosis
That's Just Not My Gift
Wags that Dog Your Tail
Then Be That Way
Where Crazies Rule the Roost

L. Richard De Prisco

YOUTUBERCULOSIS

It used to be they'd hide it all
And coop their shame up in the closet
Dirty laundry lacked the draw
In euphemism "dog deposit"
Now they drape it from the roof
Untoward junk with no restrictions
"Forward" stuff that's not a spoof
It's worse than photoshopped depictions

Don't be breathing what they air
If you can't "hack" the germs they share

To millions now all free of charge
They flaunt for public diagnosis
Gross infections they discharge
And drunk on "hits" they miss prognosis
Showing you they're living large
But such big livers risk cirrhosis
Don't contract through screens they barge
Contagious Youtuberculosis

They've done some things they'd never tape
All kept off-line from "tubies" gawking
Episodes they won't escape
Although no video they're hawking
Portals on a higher "Net"
Will shout degrading stunts they're pulling
Roof displays that none forget
Those scenes for crowds they won't be fooling

L. Richard De Prisco

Don't be breathing what they air
If you can't "hack" the germs they share

To millions now all free of charge
They flaunt for public diagnosis
Gross infections they discharge
And drunk on "hits" they miss prognosis
Showing you they're living large
But such big livers risk cirrhosis
Don't contract through screens they barge
Contagious Youtuberculosis

Just one impaneled Judge will vote
Some get His Lamb but none His goat

Events replayed in massive doses
There will show their deep neurosis
Setting fates in swift sclerosis
Curing Youtuberculosis

For further reflection:
Luke 12:2-3; 2 Cor 4:2; Phil 3:19; 2 Thes 3:11; 1 Tim 5:13; Jude 1:13

THAT'S JUST NOT MY GIFT

I've seen great faith by those so blessed
Who seem to have the knack
For swatting doubts whenever pressed
To keep belief on track
I wish my lurch to trust was swift
But that's just not my gift

The lucky ones get all the breaks
And surplus talent brings
More grants conferring what it takes
My strength's in other things
From me that paradigm did shift
As that's just not my gift

I know of some maintaining hope
When all their pillars fall
As ruin rains they never mope
Or wander from their call
My expectation's gone adrift
But that's just not my gift

The lucky ones get all the breaks
And surplus talent brings
More grants conferring what it takes
My strength's in other things
From me that paradigm did shift
As that's just not my gift

The merciful have grace to spare
So full of charity
Uncouth and charming both get care

There's no disparity
My love grows cold when there's a rift
But that's just not my gift

The lucky ones get all the breaks
And surplus talent brings
More grants conferring what it takes
My strength's in other things
From me that paradigm did shift
As that's just not my gift

Endowment's by capricious lot
And comes through sieves that sift
The chaff is all I ever got
I guess I missed that gift

The raised go up to streets of gold
But looking for that lift
To heaven's grand bequest I'm told
That that's just not my gift

For further reflection:
Matt 25:14-30; Acts 11:17; Rom 11:29, 12:6; 1 Cor 1:7, 7:7, 13:13, 14:1,
12; Eph 4:7; Phil 4:17; 1 Tim 4:14; 2 Tim 2:6; 1 Pet 4:10

WAGS THAT DOG YOUR TAIL

Legal vultures
Raspy throats denounce what ails but spew more viral cultures
Civil rulers
Praise the hotheads while they ice the righteous in their coolers

Scoffers rude and virulent
Mock the aromatic ones like hounds that find a scent

Saying nay's the only way
Jackasses have to cover tracks they're pawing as they bray
They'll bewail along your trail
So march ahead but just beware of wags that dog your tail

Guides myopic
Close their eyes to mammoth bugs but see the microscopic
Fighting forces
Gallop after phantom foes on armored hobby horses

Scoffers rude and virulent
Mock the aromatic ones like hounds that find a scent

Saying nay's the only way
Jackasses have to cover tracks they're pawing as they bray
They'll bewail along your trail
So march ahead but just beware of wags that dog your tail

Barbs bathetic
Don't feel sorry for their fall though efforts are pathetic
All their scorning
Should not move the anchored soul whose works they're just adorning

Scoffers rude and virulent
Mock the aromatic ones like hounds that find a scent

Saying nay's the only way
Jackasses have to cover tracks they're pawing as they bray
They'll bewail along your trail
So march ahead but just beware of wags that dog your tail

Such an army … cannot harm me
Easier to spot that group than if they're sweet and smarmy
Bites are toothless … from the truthless
Self-inflicted wounds all mark the cruel and the ruthless

No one's fooled … who's ridiculed
Like detractors kicked the Lord but soon their heels were cooled
Patience bogs … the critic hogs
Wait them out, those wags will turn their tails and run like dogs

For further reflection:
Job 17:2; Prov 29:8; Matt 23:24; Luke 11:53-54, 20:20, 26; 2 Pet 3:3;
Jude 1:18

THEN BE THAT WAY

Handed on a silver platter
Bon-bons that won't make you fatter
Act as if it doesn't matter
So I say … then be that way

Thinking He would soon deny us
Hold some back like Ananias
Act like martyrs harmed but pious
So I say … then be that way

I can't lift your sullen mood
Fine with me, just go and brood

What you are is what He gets
Starting fresh He re-begets
Soon He'll wipe away that pout
Frowns reverse and so do frets
Turnarounds like pirouettcs
Inward fix works right on out

Walk away from heaven's promise
Show you're hurt with melodramas
Act just like a Doubting Thomas
So I say … then be that way

Nothing being's nothing doing
Change inside by His renewing
Acting ends with full imbuing
So I say … then be that way

I can't lift your sullen mood

Fine with me, just go and brood

What you are is what He gets
Starting fresh He re-begets
Soon He'll wipe away that pout
Frowns reverse and so do frets
Turnarounds like pirouettes
Inward fix works right on out

Pointless now to moan and mope
Not a way to help you cope
All you need's a little hope

Histrionics holds no sway
Truth relay … then be that way

For further reflection:
Gen 4:5-7; Prov 23:16; John 7:38, 20:24-28; Acts 5:1-5; Eph 3:16

WHERE CRAZIES RULE THE ROOST

Just sprung from "strait" normality
I think I have a hunch
They'd "jacket" with formality
Us bozos in the bunch
Afraid to spotlight creepy sights
They think we might look weird
So all the dimwits dim their brights
When drooling hits the beard

The well-adjusted answer's pat
But I'll keep screaming nuts to that

The sober-faced should be restrained
Just run from them and seek
Asylum from the highly "saned"
All lingerers will freak
Golgotha gives ghoul-gothic scare
Where foamy mouths are juiced
But I would feel much safer there
Where crazies rule the roost

The ones who speak of sacrifice
And weakness making strong
Get padded rooms where muzak's nice
Though wardens there belong
The inmates, brave and blessing, come
No chickens with a pox
Their cup's half-fool, but not so dumb
They're crazy like a fox

The well-adjusted answer's pat

But I'll keep screaming nuts to that

The sober-faced should be restrained
Just run from them and seek
Asylum from the highly "saned"
All lingerers will freak
Golgotha gives ghoul-gothic scare
Where foamy mouths are juiced
But I would feel much safer there
Where crazies rule the roost

His therapy won't straighten hair
No shocks are introduced
There won't be some electric chair
Where currents are induced

His institution for our care
Will let our tongues be loosed
When Jesus meets us in the air
We crazies get a boost

For further reflection:
1 Sam 21:13; 2 Sam 8:15; Mark 3:21; Luke 1:64; John 10:20; 1 Cor
1:18-29, 4:9-10; 2 Cor 11:1, 17, 21, 23, 30, 12:6, 11; 1 Thes 4:17

Chapter 8

Frayed So

Wolves' Clothing
If You Can?
One Sky's Falling at a Time
Crawling Butterflies
Acrophobic, Falling

WOLVES' CLOTHING

From there inside it chafes a bit
That fur can itch much worse than wool
You can't expect a perfect fit
That crouch you try does not look cool
The crowd you keep keeps wary eye
On sheepish grins all rather wan
Their menu makes them wonder why
It's meadow grass you're dining on

Wolves' clothing just is not your style
So who gets fooled by chintzy guile?

Your whiter coat you under-wear
And overdress with silly pelt
That heavy wrap's just plunder fare
Since with your kind you've poorly dealt
In photo ops you give a scare
In backgrounds gray you meekly melt
To walk with kin you'd never dare
And with those flocks you've never knelt

You think protection there is best
The alpha male will watch your back
Until the "rolling over" test
When tummy views suggest a snack
The Shepherd proves a better lead
But glares at you across the way
Perhaps you'll now begin to plead
You've failed in learning how to "prey"

Wolves' clothing just is not your style

So who gets fooled by chintzy guile?

Your whiter coat you under-wear
And overdress with silly pelt
That heavy wrap's just plunder fare
Since with your kind you've poorly dealt
In photo ops you give a scare
In backgrounds gray you meekly melt
To walk with kin you'd never dare
And with those flocks you've never knelt

When carnivores would prowl your beat
It never works to growl your bleat

So leave the pack, rejoin your group
Don't "hang with fang," you're not that beast
You can't maintain that "hair"-brained dupe
You're better off just getting fleeced

For further reflection:
Matt 7:15, 10:16; Mark 14:66-72; John 10:11-15; Rom 12:2;
Gal 2:11-14; 1 Pet 1:14-15

IF YOU CAN?

Come inside and dwell within
"Will you let Me serve your sentence?"
Yes! I'll turn from all my sin
Lord, please help my unrepentance!

Plow and furrow all my field
"Will you give your heart as tender?"
Yes! I'll bow and fully yield
Lord, please help my unsurrender!

All of me believes You can
But part of me says, no You can't
Take the weakness from this man
Instill assurance that You'll grant
All the things I sorely need
Full faith is Your essential plan
Would the birds ask as they feed
… "If You can"?

Soften up this neck, subdue
"Will you end your stiff defiance?"
Yes! I'll fully lean on You
Lord, please help my unreliance!

Take my envy – had my fill
"Will you lose your fierce resentment?"
Yes! I'll rest inside Your will
Lord, please help my uncontentment!

All of me believes You can
But part of me says, no You can't
Take the weakness from this man

Instill assurance that You'll grant
All the things I sorely need
Full faith is Your essential plan
Would the birds ask as they feed
… "If You can"?

Let me know Your love's complete; suspend and end this undependence
Wash me, clean these dusty feet; suspend and end this unresplendence
Give me wings for higher flights; suspend and end this unascendance
Train me here to tread the heights; suspend and end this untranscendence

Send these troubling doubts away
"Will you let Me start relieving?"
Yes! I'll trust each word You say
Lord, please help my unbelieving!

For further reflection:
2 Chron 30:8; Mark 9:20-24; Luke 12:22-24; Rom 2:4-5;
1 Tim 6:6; Jas 4:7

ONE SKY'S FALLING AT A TIME

My world came caving in today
Slow motion clips of disarray
Like shrapnel spreading in a spray
I've come unglued
A whistling heralds second round
That detonates with piercing sound
No standing remnants can be found
Since burns ensued

And thinking I've endured the worst
I find this wave is just the first
Of more to burst

It seems it's more than I can take
I watch disasters get in line
They make my deep foundations shake
But whispers say that none are mine
By some ironic paradigm
Though when it rains it always pours
Just one sky's falling at a time
And now I see that each one's Yours

This world is but my oyster shell
It's not my paradise or hell
An alternate runs parallel
With bigger stakes
Explosions there were far more shrill
They bought a peace that's calmer still
And all these craters will refill
For heaven's sakes

And thinking I've endured the worst
I find this wave is just the first
Of more to burst

It seems it's more than I can take
I watch disasters get in line
They make my deep foundations shake
But whispers say that none are mine
By some ironic paradigm
Though when it rains it always pours
Just one sky's falling at a time
And now I see that each one's Yours

No sky drops more than I can bear
I'm kept from all the brutal brunts
You've borne the burden's weighty share
And raised the pieces all at once

For further reflection:
Matt 16:2-3, 24:29-31; 1 Cor 10:13; Heb 12:3; Rev 11:6

CRAWLING BUTTERFLIES

With lifeless blue the dull sky drones
Uninterrupted monotones
Bright palette streaks remain unknowns
No tempera warms temperate zones

For such a worm as I once was
This newborn is what airborne does

Though churning in my inward parts
I've got no stomach for these guys
Their take-offs stall in fits and starts
And rarely will they flit and rise
To flutter, float, then zoom in darts
They freeze from sprawling, utter lies
I stare at grounded, failing hearts
Entranced by crawling butterflies

They shuffle in their wingtip shoes
Just creeping like mere men who choose
Low profiles over higher views
All flights so fancy they'd refuse

For such a worm as I once was
This newborn is what airborne does

Though churning in my inward parts
I've got no stomach for these guys
Their take-offs stall in fits and starts
And rarely will they flit and rise
To flutter, float, then zoom in darts
They freeze from sprawling, utter lies

I stare at grounded, failing hearts
Entranced by crawling butterflies

By clinging to their earthly post
On lifting winds they cannot coast

This chrysalis once had its place
For metamorphic episode
But once cocoons have empty space
Their contents upward must explode

For further reflection:
Psa 55:6; Isa 40:29-31; 1 Cor 3:1-4; Heb 5:12-6:2

ACROPHOBIC, FALLING

Once enthroned on highchair seat
Ruling over all I saw
Throwing food was such a treat
Quarters cramped, the only flaw
'Til I took a sudden gander down along the side
And noticed with a drop that I'd be in for quite a ride
Then I cried …

Get me loose but set me gently on the floor
Need room to move but mainly ground that's safe and sure

Cooped up looking for a hatch and gropin'
I, a claustrophobic crawling,
Found the fuselage with bay doors open
Now I'm acrophobic, falling

Tilt no paths when I'm on edge
Missing guardrails make me freeze
Views are awesome from the ledge
What will happen if I sneeze?
Quick acceleration downward with a force of g
Goes through my one-track mind in slow-mo "high" anxiety
Hear my plea …

Get me loose but set me gently on the floor
Need room to move but mainly ground that's safe and sure

Cooped up looking for a hatch and gropin'
I, a claustrophobic crawling,
Found the fuselage with bay doors open
Now I'm acrophobic, falling

Strangled here inside this stifling box now closing in
Panic-seized
Scared to open arms to grab the ones You'll wrap me in
Danger's eased

Terrors of hard crashes and impending doom just melt
When I see Your smiling face
Now I trip on purpose into love my heart has felt
Everything just falls in place

For further reflection:
Deut 33:27; 2 Sam 22:34; Psa 66:9, 118:13; Hab 3:19; Matt 21:44

Chapter 9

Rough and Stumble

Male Pattern Boldness
Nope, Just Can't, Sir
Mighty Servant Girl
Warriors in Therapy
Leave the Old Man There to Rot

L. Richard De Prisco

MALE PATTERN BOLDNESS

Young hooligans saw thinning hair
In bald-faced scheme for big crowd-pleaser
Rushing where no angels dare
To mock and taunt the prophet geezer
One-upped by a female bear
Whose deep-bass grunts were not a teaser

Masculine is force containment
Unlike boasts preposterous
Measured steps mean true attainment
Not just bursts testosterous

Our Warrior came mild and meek
With "Ancient" roots from days of "oldness"
Loving but with judgments bleak
Mistaken for some inner coldness
Gentle strength, no hints of weak
Are signs that show male pattern boldness

The sissy label's hard to stick
Atop a still but steely tower
Peaceful feet are made to kick
And march when tenderfoots just cower
Wings that guard the frailest chick:
Unflappable almighty power

Masculine is force containment
Unlike boasts preposterous
Measured steps mean true attainment
Not just bursts testosterous

Our Warrior came mild and meek
With "Ancient" roots from days of "oldness"
Loving but with judgments bleak
Mistaken for some inner coldness
Gentle strength, no hints of weak
Are signs that show male pattern boldness

When discretion makes for valor
Men are men with no excuse
Some misjudged One's ashen pallor
But from death He's broken loose

They guessed He lacked that "virile" gland
And thought He'd coddle whiny peasants
'Til they heard that fierce command
"Now slay them right here in My presence"

For further reflection:
2 Kings 2:23-24; Dan 7:9-14; Matt 23:37; Mark 15:31-32;
Luke 19:11-27; 2 Cor 10:1-2

NOPE, JUST CAN'T, SIR

I can think what more I'd do if I were always healthy
But His wise objective:
More dependence lest I get too independent, wealthy
That my work's defective
With regret He sends regards by messengers so stealthy
Sickness is protective

He must check metastasizing disobedience
Means are always in accord with His expedience

What to me are Satan's tools are godly for prevention
Scalpels and the lancer
"Would you take without revolt the thing I dare not mention?
Contemplate your answer
Can you think what else gets undivided full attention?"
I said, "Nope, just can't, Sir"

When I turn malignant I am apt to start complaining
Show how bad I'm feeling
Surgery will follow since those deadly cells need draining
Chemo leaves me reeling
But He uses anesthetics when my nerves are straining
Balms He'll use for healing

He must check metastasizing disobedience
Means are always in accord with His expedience

What to me are Satan's tools are godly for prevention
Scalpels and the lancer
"Would you take without revolt the thing I dare not mention?
Contemplate your answer

Can you think what else gets undivided full attention?"
I said, "Nope, just can't, Sir"

Clean will be my bill of health – it goes with my adoption
Ills now mediation
But for my severe disease He'll implement this option:
Love as radiation

"Malady is what I use so often by convention
'Righteousness enhancer'
Do you see alternatives to counter My intention?"
Can't He go with, "Can't, Sir"?

For further reflection:
Ruth 1:21; 2 Chron 16:12; Psa 106:15; Prov 18:14; Isa 10:16;
Ezek 34:4; 2 Cor 12:7-9

MIGHTY SERVANT GIRL

Brute elephants will rush, stampede
Their fearless rage no flood could douse
The wildest beast could not impede
Their rash assault … except a mouse
It seems the brave are quick to rise
And face fierce foes when odds are long
Against the titans fury flies
But paired with weak they're not so strong

When cowards don't the daring do
Still bent on more heroic feats
You feel their boldness burning through
And cut off all your known retreats
With nerves of steel unlike the rest
Where dread makes others' eyebrows curl
But when raw courage puffs your chest
Beware the mighty servant girl

A fisherman would mock the storm
And wield his sword when armies came
Since danger was the daily norm
And life and death were all the same
Prepared to battle frightful things
He'd taken on each Philistine
Like shepherd boy who toyed with slings
Yet scared to death to make a scene

When cowards don't the daring do
Still bent on more heroic feats
You feel their boldness burning through
And cut off all your known retreats

With nerves of steel unlike the rest
Where dread makes others' eyebrows curl
But when raw courage puffs your chest
Beware the mighty servant girl

On potent fiends all oversized
The valiant one will set his sight
The tiny leave him paralyzed
And meekly have him put to flight

To dash in two each monster threat
Their unprotected bodies hurl
With caution thrown their jaws are set
Until they meet the servant girl

For further reflection:
1 Sam 17:34-37; Matt 14:28-29, 16:21-22, 26:69-74;
Luke 22:56-60; John 18:10

WARRIORS IN THERAPY

The world has launched a volley of demeaning mocking taunts
And casualties are carried from a trench's blasted haunts
On "stretchers" of their faith they're laid though bones are all intact
They thought they'd died for sure but recollection's not exact

Recruits in boot camp once were told this fight's no piece of cake
The bayonet of cutting words carves many in its wake
Each time they feel their face get red they think they're losing blood
And when they see their pride pour out the tears begin to flood

The counselors are lining up all white in buttoned coats
As talking wounded spill their guts and fill up pads of notes
Some jots are scribbled, meds prescribed, each time they're crying,
    "Ouch!"
As warriors in therapy get time out on the couch

It's true that some are really maimed and need some urgent care
Conditions rated serious should always trump the fair
The hangnail hurts will heal in time but soldiers have a job
To man the battle lines despite the minor painful throb

Some persecution must arise for strikers on the front
Their Sergeant's felt the worst Himself and all their blows He'll blunt
They can't expect a cozy scrap when carrying a cross
But rolling on just like their Rock they must not gather moss

The counselors are lining up all white in buttoned coats
As talking wounded spill their guts and fill up pads of notes
Some jots are scribbled, meds prescribed, each time they're crying,
    "Ouch!"
As warriors in therapy get time out on the couch

Exhorting all to courage He gives orders not to fear
His privates feel a glancing shot but not a piercing spear
The bullets that their foes are shooting ricochet away
No arsenal can penetrate protection built to stay

A final perseverance holds His loved ones facing darts
Through armored suits no mortal hits can get to vital parts
But scratches often bring on howls from all the weaker links
If only they could recognize His Shield took all the chinks

The counselors are lining up all white in buttoned coats
As talking wounded spill their guts and fill up pads of notes
Some jots are scribbled, meds prescribed, each time they're crying,
    "Ouch!"
As warriors in therapy get time out on the couch

His troops survive the conflict here, their Leader rescues all
Retreats for scrapes and bruises though means skirmishes could stall
The war goes on so technically each PTSD claim
Means brief removal of that "post" (unless His Kingdom came)

For further reflection:
Josh 1:6-9; Matt 5:10, 10:38; John 15:20; 1 Cor 4:11-13; 2 Cor 4:8-11;
Gal 6:12; Eph 6:10-17; 2 Tim 2:3, 3:12, 4:5-7; Heb 10:39, 12:3-13;
1 John 2:28; Rev 21:8

LEAVE THE OLD MAN THERE TO ROT

They all just saw one body there
Attention rightly fixed on Him
Spectators then were not aware
This second man was not a whim
And not the Holy Ghost I mean
That "hanger-on" was one I know
Another thief was at the scene
Though flesh and blood would never show

They took the Savior down that night
A specter stayed there nailed up tight

He saw the resurrection come
And wishes now to come alive
But I know where he's coming from
To keep him there I now must strive
The Roman legion should have stayed
To guard that "post" but they would not
The duty's mine, for strength I've prayed
To leave the old man there to rot

But every now and then he jumps
And sets his tree flat on the ground
I put him back to take his lumps
A daily chore as I have found
The trouble is he had no grave
No stone to keep him trapped inside
But soon he'll hold no hostage slave
When flesh he steals has finally died

They took the Savior down that night
A specter stayed there nailed up tight

He saw the resurrection come
And wishes now to come alive
But I know where he's coming from
To keep him there I now must strive
The Roman legion should have stayed
To guard that "post" but they would not
The duty's mine, for strength I've prayed
To leave the old man there to rot

We long were friends and shared a lot
A better One is what I've got
Decrepit one I pity not
And shed no tears to see him rot

For further reflection:
Luke 9:23; Rom 6:6-11, 8:10; Gal 2:20, 5:24, 6:14; Eph 4:22; Col 3:5-9

Chapter 10

Maker's Prerogative

He Thought, Therefore I Am
Who's to Blame?
Called Every Name in the Book
Velvet Ultimatum

L. Richard De Prisco

HE THOUGHT, THEREFORE I AM

I thought they think He thought, you think?
The light came on in just a blink
I gave Him back a knowing wink
He didn't raise a stink
With no existence, how'd I know?
From where I came, to where I'll go
I bet you think I'm really slow
Intelligence will show

If no perception hits the brain
Then how can thought maintain its train?

How could I know I'm really here?
Not just illusion so unclear
Am I a figment, should I fear?
Imagination's queer
If it's a joke it's quite a scam
My idcation is a sham
Can I be more than just a clam?
He thought, therefore I am

My mind can play some dirty tricks
But consciousness still has the fix
Remember no forgetting sticks
The two will never mix
So contemplate yourself a while
Your intellect's cerebral pile
Knows what philosophies to file
It thinks, Cartesian-style

If no perception hits the brain
Then how can thought maintain its train?

How could I know I'm really here?
Not just illusion so unclear
Am I a figment, should I fear?
Imagination's queer
If it's a joke it's quite a scam
My ideation is a sham
Can I be more than just a clam?
He thought, therefore I am

My ruminations are a clue
No apparition's fooling you

He cogitates reality
It's what I thought, I think I see
I'm glad He thought kind thoughts of me
He thinks, therefore I'll be

For further reflection:
Job 12:7-10; Psa 40:5, 92:5, 139:14-17; Rom 1:19-22, 11:33;
1 Cor 2:10-16

WHO'S TO BLAME?

Discrepancies like weeds unsown
Crop up where fallow fields are grown
And left alone they go to seed
Where hungry flocks are prone to feed
It's not as if the sorting's hard
For lack of workers in the yard
No shifts are left without a guard

But every time there's something wrong
And lists of ills are getting long
Behind it vetoes are withheld
Before a single tree is felled
Or merciless can kill and maim
Disgruntled then are apt to frame
The One who's surely not to blame

To Him they'd fain attribute guilt
A tribute to some straw men built
Yet often there is none to fault
Despite the deaf and blind and halt
The Righteous Branch Himself once died
So sinners have no place to hide
From fair misfortunes all decried

But every time there's something wrong
And lists of ills are getting long
Behind it vetoes are withheld
Before a single tree is felled
Or merciless can kill and maim
Disgruntled then are apt to frame
The One who's surely not to blame

Each text is authored with the quill
Of players writing out their will
And though ordained they script their game
Revealing clearly who's to blame
By acts disclosing they agree
With verdicts they refuse to see
Confessed by mute apology

But every time there's something wrong
And lists of ills are getting long
Behind it vetoes are withheld
Before a single tree is felled
Or merciless can kill and maim
Disgruntled then are apt to frame
The One who's surely not to blame

The force that has them all unnerved
Is freedom to themselves reserved
But choosing to renounce their choice
Condemning by their very voice
The faculty from whence it came
They forfeit powers to declaim
Whose right to judge and whose to blame

For further reflection:
Job 33:13, 36:3; Psa 92:15; Isa 40:13-14, 45:9; Lam 3:39-40; John 9:1-3;
Rom 9:19-21

CALLED EVERY NAME IN THE BOOK

They're compounding surnames to honor both sides
The tree branches bend from ancestral divides
But what it you're first in the line at the trunk?
You'd still add your hyphens for roots that you've sunk

Jehovah's got add-ons for roles that He plays
There's "Rapha" to show that He's healed all our ways
And "Jireh" reveals He provides for His own
While "Nissi" His banner's for altars of stone

Forget all of these if you're not good at names
Just not "Late For Sinner" or flippant "Home, James"

Repentance with faith is the key that applies
A garbled up moniker He won't despise
Pronounce them however you can, but true cries
For mercy He never mistook
A simple "God, help!" bends His ear to your pleas
The state of the heart, not the title, He sees
So call out the handle that suits you since He's
Been called every name in the Book

"Tsidkenu's" a tongue-twist for pure righteousness
"Shammah" means He's present (and voting, no less)
As "Ra-ah" the Shepherd He watches His fleece
"Shalom" gives us comfort since He is our peace

Familiar addresses don't need a kibosh
Respect that He's holy (to Jews that's "Kadosh")
For reverence Israel once had an eye
They uttered as sacred the name "Adonai"

Forget all of these if you're not good at names
Just not "Late For Sinner" or flippant "Home, James"

Repentance with faith is the key that applies
A garbled up moniker He won't despise
Pronounce them however you can, but true cries
For mercy He never mistook
A simple "God, help!" bends His ear to your pleas
The state of the heart, not the title, He sees
So call out the handle that suits you since He's
Been called every name in the Book

The choices are many, be bold, don't go stealth
Just pick one when needing some heavenly wealth
Just never in vain (if you're watching your health)

For further reflection:
Gen 22:14; Exo 15:26, 17:15; Judg 6:24; Psa 23:1; Isa 12:6; Jer 23:6;
Ezek 48:35; Matt 15:25

VELVET ULTIMATUM

What packaging would suit your skin
Which tears apart when strung so taut?
You've kept it safe, though paper-thin,
From paper cuts, or so you thought
But puncture wounds once had their day
They made their mark, their work is done
Their message comes another way
Until you choose it hasn't won

Who'd propose to draw the blind
With tones of voice increasing?
Urgency is not defined
By high-pitched threats policing
Don't regard His softness as
Inconsequential datum
Feel the weight His warning has
In velvet ultimatum

The gauntlet laid is not the kind
Like "it's your money or your life"
Nor hostage-takers in a bind
Who force a choice of kids or wife
There is an up-side in this mix
Just run the table in the match
There's no "lose-lose" or dirty tricks
You'll lose it all, though, if you "scratch"

Who'd propose to draw the blind
With tones of voice increasing?
Urgency is not defined
By high-pitched threats policing

Don't regard His softness as
Inconsequential datum
Feel the weight His warning has
In velvet ultimatum

Delicate but hard as rocks
Don't let that satin fool you
Gently teaching hardest knocks
With tenderness to school you

Not a cloth you'd want to strip
I wouldn't try to bait Him
Careful now, don't fray or rip
His velvet ultimatum

For further reflection:
Exo 34:6-7; Rom 2:4-10, 3:25, 9:22, 11:22; 1 Pet 3:20; 2 Pet 3:9, 15

Chapter 11

Winning the Appeal Process

Genius with Three Wishes
Wisdom for Dummies
Lady of the Golden Streets
Confessions of a Holy Man
Soft Apocalypse
Carpe Deum

L. Richard De Prisco

GENIUS WITH THREE WISHES

So dumb to think I knew … Well, what would genius do? ….

I gathered that my wits were quick
In gathering intelligence all bottled up inside
A head-lamp rub was just the trick
And out came foggy genius with three wishes all supplied

At first I marveled at my luck
And wished I had more time to think to let the options flow
Then right away the deal was struck
My genius said the time was mine, two wishes now to go

Unnumbered are my daily hopes
So many now a dime a dozen's just ten cents too much
If I could just use periscopes
From wishing wells I've fallen in no wishes would I clutch
(That wish is unofficial!
I know: it's superficial)
My genius with three wishes says my dreams are out of touch

More shrewd with second thoughts in mind
I wished to see the future so I'd know what would be done
I hate this navigating blind
He said I'll see it when it comes, and now I'm down to one

Determined not to waste the last
I wished for ten more wishes so I'd have a few to blow
My genius wished me well and cast
Those ten to me but said their *granting's* not for him to throw

Unnumbered are my daily hopes

So many now a dime a dozen's just ten cents too much
If I could just use periscopes
From wishing wells I've fallen in no wishes would I clutch
(That wish is unofficial!
I know: it's superficial)
My genius with three wishes says my dreams are out of touch

If wishes were like drops of rain
I still would never have enough to change a single hair
But with each one's the same refrain:
I wish I had just one more wish, that's all I want, I swear!

I pondered long in my despair
And sharpened up my keenest smarts to clean out all the fuzz
I wish I'd put my wants to prayer
I've learned the hard way in my loss that that's what genius does

For further reflection:
Matt 15:28, 21:22; Mark 10:35-40, 11:24; John 15:7; Jas 4:3;
1 John 5:14-15

WISDOM FOR DUMMIES

It's bound not to come when you open your trap
It's bound in a pamphlet-size book
It's found in few words that could fit on the flap
It's founded on truth some mistook

Some wordless articulate loftiest themes
Some "worthless" propound what redeems

Those fools are thought wise when they listen, not speak
Those tools giving simple great skill
Those schools remain open for all who would seek
Those rules that make ignorance nil

It's ground for more grace from proverbial seer
It's ground in that pestle of quips
It's sound when it starts with a reverent fear
It's sounded on whispers of lips

Some wordless articulate loftiest themes
Some "worthless" propound what redeems

Those fools are thought wise when they listen, not speak
Those tools giving simple great skill
Those schools remain open for all who would seek
Those rules that make ignorance nil

Now sowing with seeds that from heaven have rained
Now growing with grace these shine through
Now showing with brilliance the wisdom they've gained
Now knowing with insight what's true

Some wordless articulate loftiest themes
Some "worthless" propound what redeems

Those fools are thought wise when they listen, not speak
Those tools giving simple great skill
Those schools remain open for all who would seek
Those rules that make ignorance nil

The ray of bright light will exalt the untaught
The day that they open their eyes
The gray of the dullest will fade if He's sought
The way that the dumb become wise

For further reflection:
Prov 4:7, 8:5, 9:10, 10:19, 11:2, 13:10, 15:33, 17:28; Luke 21:14-15;
Jas 1:5

LADY OF THE GOLDEN STREETS

The woman of my wildest dreams
That's not what I first took her as
Her face so plain but still it beams
I've long been craving what she has

She wasn't shy but gave me looks
To draw me in from off the streets
I'm starving for the feasts she cooks
It's just for her my heart still beats

So chase this chaste one, kings and pawns
She chastens not the one who fawns

She walks the alleys in the night
Where no disease or blinding blight
Will sicken like the paramour
The whitest light's above her door
You'll find discernment in her eyes
And knowledge not like worldly wise
This wizened woman never cheats
This lady of the golden streets

Some stand her up, she stands them down
She has no use for cat-like calls
It's fools who mock her rich renown
It's by her lights one stands or falls

So chase this chaste one, kings and pawns
She chastens not the one who fawns

She walks the alleys in the night

Where no disease or blinding blight
Will sicken like the paramour
The whitest light's above her door
You'll find discernment in her eyes
And knowledge not like worldly wise
This wizened woman never cheats
This lady of the golden streets

It's wisdom in her golden dress
The prudent long for her caress

All lovers now her song entreats
She welcomes any friend she meets
And once they find her in those streets
They'll sit with her on golden seats

For further reflection:
Prov 1:20-33, 2:10-19, 3:13-18, 8:1-9:6

CONFESSIONS OF A HOLY MAN

If you would scale a craggy peak
I'm not the guru that you seek
No shaman telling you up front
Skip Ganges dip and dervish stunt
If ayatollah told you so
Address is wrong, you're free to go
The garb and bling are not my thing
No angel carols 'round me ring

But if it's sacred text you need
I'm authorized, dispensing creed

I'll tell you here with full disclosure
Imperfections mark my trail
No intricate detailed exposure
Makes me lose in pass-or-fail
So don't be swayed by worst impressions
Needless now to poke and prod
These pure expressions mark confessions
Of a holy man of God

The sins I've known would make you faint
But none disqualify this saint
No Spartan settings help my cause
I operate by other laws
Transgressions meet impunity
I'm granted full immunity
While flaws of mine are myriad
It's His credentials, period

But if it's sacred text you need

I'm authorized, dispensing creed

I'll tell you here with full disclosure
Imperfections mark my trail
No intricate detailed exposure
Makes me lose in pass-or-fail
So don't be swayed by worst impressions
Needless now to poke and prod
These pure expressions mark confessions
Of a holy man of God

Asceticism's not on trial
Not the point of self-denial

Though inner change must surely show
There's just one thing I'd have you know
He's wholly God and wholly man
Which I confess … His holy man

For further reflection:
Rom 10:8-10, 11:16; 1 Cor 3:17; Eph 1:4, 2:21, 5:27; Col 1:22; 1 Pet 2:9

SOFT APOCALYPSE

I've known a scathing wind to howl
Is this the way You'd sweep me off my feet?
It might evince an angry scowl
Much calmer air from You I would entreat

If massifs crumble all around
Would rending rocks suffice to break my will?
I'd feel as if I'm losing ground
To moles that turn my mountains to a hill

Still waiting for the other shoe to drop
I see You're barefoot when the terrors stop
How many feet are in that yard of Yours?
My confidence that lighter step restores

Your power's more than I could gauge
If trembling hands could measure such displays
Catastrophes might show Your rage
But cowering, I couldn't stand Your ways
I'll die if You show no restraint
My mortal fear Your fiercest fury whips
Reveal too much and see me faint
So come to me in soft apocalypse

When flames are racing uncontrolled
They sear a vision of Gehenna's heat
Those scorching embers leave me cold
And frenzied wrath is all I'd exegete

Still waiting for the other shoe to drop
I see You're barefoot when the terrors stop

How many feet are in that yard of Yours?
My confidence that lighter step restores

Your power's more than I could gauge
If trembling hands could measure such displays
Catastrophes might show Your rage
But cowering, I couldn't stand Your ways
I'll die if You show no restraint
My mortal fear Your fiercest fury whips
Reveal too much and see me faint
So come to me in soft apocalypse

So is the tenor of Your voice still small?
For me that speaks the loudest after all

With eyes restored from brutal blinding light
I'm coming gently into this good night

For further reflection:
1 Kings 19:9-14; Matt 21:5; 1 Thes 2:7-8; Rev 8:1-4

CARPE DEUM

All access lanes are crowded
People jammed up close
The entryways are shrouded
Hurdles by the gross
The sight lines left are clouded
All morale's morose

One narrow window's cracked a smidge
It just might be your only bridge

You've waited for that passing chance
And found that happy happenstance
So strike without a second glance
Seize the moment … play the man
It might not linger very long
This pathway through the pressing throng
Just grab the ring and hold on strong
Carpe Deum … while you can

A green light quickly flashes
Got to make some moves
The wise will make mad dashes
Showing they've got hooves
His gates are made for crashes
Door ajar just proves

One narrow window's cracked a smidge
It just might be your only bridge

You've waited for that passing chance
And found that happy happenstance

So strike without a second glance
Seize the moment … play the man
It might not linger very long
This pathway through the pressing throng
Just grab the ring and hold on strong
Carpe Deum … while you can

If all you grasp is just the hem
You could just find you've clutched a gem

It's time to run with all dispatch
Then reach your hand to make a snatch
The God you brush you'll never catch
Carpe Deum … while you can

For further reflection:
Isa 55:6; Matt 11:12, 20:30-34; Mark 2:2-5; Luke 8:42-48, 19:2-9;
Acts 17:27

Chapter 12

The Fix is In

Broken Dishes
Healing Lame Excuses
Levi's Genes
Orthodox Orthotics
Like CPR for Corpses

L. Richard De Prisco

BROKEN DISHES

In just a flash it turned to waste
Delectables so neatly placed
Now scattered far across the floor
Return to scratch and start once more

What's served on top may be top choice
But lacking serving vehicle
Gourmets unfed cannot rejoice
Or rate the sweetest treacle

It always seems the product valued
Disregards the carrier
But should you learn it never shall you'd
Never be a barrier
So voice to Him new spoken wishes
For delivery when you pray
Please mend us all, Your broken dishes
So Your works might find display

The picture was so sharply clear
Then suddenly a fuzzy smear
The satellite had signaled well
But its receiver could not tell

What's channeled down may be top rate
But lacking working medium
All viewers find there while they wait
Upon repairs, pure tedium

It always seems the product valued
Disregards the carrier

But should you learn it never shall you'd
Never be a barrier
So voice to Him new spoken wishes
For delivery when you pray
Please mend us all, Your broken dishes
So Your works might find display

The apparatus plays a role
Ascribing honor's never droll

He's cleaning up some soakin' dishes
Good as new they're back in play
Presentable for broken fishes
Ones on roofs collect each ray

For further reflection:
Job 10:9; Lam 4:2; Rom 9:22-23; 2 Cor 4:7; 2 Tim 2:20

HEALING LAME EXCUSES

Amazing they don't tear the roof
Or push through crowds to touch a fringe
They barely loiter all aloof
His look their way just made them cringe
No convalescence would they seek
Their need for treatment they disguise
They drink elixirs really weak
Libations made of alibis

Recoiling from the great Physician
They'll forgo His deft incision

Open wounds they leave to fester
Guarding those they love to nurse
For miracles they never pester
And to cures they seem averse
So masochistic for abuses
They prefer what they can see
But when He's healing lame excuses
Clinics have some vacancy

Quite happy they endure the pain
Their analgesics mask the hurt
They're saying, "Let me just explain"
But their dismissals seem too curt
They've got good reasons to decline
Or so they say when they are pressed
They wince protesting they are fine
Their legion lesions never dressed

Recoiling from the great Physician
They'll forgo His deft incision

Open wounds they leave to fester
Guarding those they love to nurse
For miracles they never pester
And to cures they seem averse
So masochistic for abuses
They prefer what they can see
But when He's healing lame excuses
Clinics have some vacancy

With legs all shriveled from disuse
On crutches hobbling still obtuse

Discounting mortal sores they try
To bandage gashes with their talk
They've made their bed but there they lie
They need to take it up and walk

For further reflection:
Matt 13:15; Mark 2:4, 17; Luke 8:43-44, 14:16-24; John 15:22;
Rom 1:20, 2:1

LEVI'S GENES

I've never seen an ephod
Just not the kind of thing you find in any swank department store
I haven't touched a laver
And sacrificing animals has never been my favorite chore

Perhaps I'm all washed up but here a sacred rite
Is what I'm serving in this temple day and night
By sacrificing fragrant praises left and right

I'm in the 'hood that Levi's tribe once founded
A royal priesthood where the roles are grounded
In altar work a higher Priest got chartered
Genetic lines from precious blood He bartered
Descended through a Spirit link
To consecrated clan I think
I'm dressed in Levi's genes I'm guaranteed will never shrink

I get incensed whenever
I see some smoke go up to soothe an angry soul with just a whiff
If waving grain's a duty
I think I'll waive the ceremony of the somber and the stiff

Perhaps I'm all washed up but here a sacred rite
Is what I'm serving in this temple day and night
By sacrificing fragrant praises left and right

I'm in the 'hood that Levi's tribe once founded
A royal priesthood where the roles are grounded
In altar work a higher Priest got chartered
Genetic lines from precious blood He bartered
Descended through a Spirit link

To consecrated clan I think
I'm dressed in Levi's genes I'm guaranteed will never shrink

These genes'll never make me blue
And yeah, they all come Stone-washed too
Melchizedek's got genes to trade
But you won't ever see them fade

For further reflection:
Heb 6:20, 7:11-19; 1 Pet 2:9; Rev 5:9-10, 20:6

ORTHODOX ORTHOTICS

Your gait is open, pigeon-toed
So trips from here to there are slowed
That limping keeps you off your pace
You're praising cane, but losing place

You're listing left, now walk upright
From toe to shin pull laces tight
It's all in how your dogs are shod
With dogma loose you barely plod

You'd like to be so dutiful
With feet of peace so beautiful

The feats designed are much too hard
For races no robotics run
Your speed those crippling creeds retard
Have orthodox orthotics done

You need to "heel," get custom shoes
It's not some petty cure you'd choose
With worn-out "soul" you're out of pep
Your "tongue" is tied and not "in step"

Whenever you feel arches fall
A crack Podiatrist on call
Can have His expertise applied
So you can take it all in stride

You'd like to be so dutiful
With feet of peace so beautiful

The feats designed are much too hard
For races no robotics run
Your speed those crippling creeds retard
Have orthodox orthotics done

Ignoring pain won't get you through
Forget the role narcotics played
When weakened doctrines hobble you
Get orthodox orthotics made

For further reflection:
Deut 5:32-33; Rom 10:15; Eph 6:15; 1 Tim 6:3-5; 2 Tim 4:3-4

LIKE CPR FOR CORPSES

When walls are bricked the reason's clear
And banging heads won't make the list
Those traffic spikes don't help you steer
They're not for traction (get the gist?)

That pepper spray is not for steaks
You aim it wrong and take your licks
A jailer bribed means "that's the breaks"
And truncheons make poor pick-up sticks

For most things with utility
Misuses breed futility

Like water on a petrol blaze
Or cutting ties to join the club
Like sunscreen for a lunar phase
And temperance meetings at the pub
Like break dance gigs to stop the rain
And crocheted cups that serve no good
To die for life might be in vain
Like CPR for corpses would

A fishing hook might snag your back
Bad casting call could make fish laugh
But one mistake there won't mean jack
The joke's on them when there's a "gaffe"

A withered branch should feel the saw
To save the tree with prospects slim
Unless the rot's a fatal flaw
Or sawyer's out there on the limb

For most things with utility
Misuses breed futility

Like water on a petrol blaze
Or cutting ties to join the club
Like sunscreen for a lunar phase
And temperance meetings at the pub
Like break dance gigs to stop the rain
And crocheted cups that serve no good
To die for life might be in vain
Like CPR for corpses would

The Master Doctor's plan is brash
In vivifying lifeless trash
He lubes dry bones all bleached to ash
A reassembly from the crash

That "Cardio" has lots of heart
His pulmonary puff gives breath
Resuscitation's made a start
The life that's "pumped" springs back from death

For further reflection:
Ezek 36:26, 37:1-10; Hag 1:6; John 20:22; Rom 5:7-8, 6:3-11

Chapter 13

Fun-Trick Ponies

X-Word Puzzle
Eight Lives Down
Well, I Never ... !
Nine in Ten Agree
Unsalty Salt
Poetic Mercy

L. Richard De Prisco

X-WORD PUZZLE

(Note: the "puzzle" both named – in capital letters – and performed in the second stanza is carried out again in both "Reassembly" refrain versions on a larger scale.)

Do you 'C' what you 'R' since His word has been spoken?
'O' try to 'S' 'S' all the damage He's broken
But some shun the Name and the instrument standing
As symbol of all the redemption commanding

[CROSSOVER:]

Substitute mark to replace the dear Name?
Out of convenience or maybe from shame?

But the letter that's used only accents what's hidden
It points to the work from their lips they've forbidden
Man SCRAMBLES to skip and expunge holy label
To CRAM in his blight, not to BLESS when he's able

[CROSSOVER]

[REASSEMBLY #1:]

WE LOOK TO THIS CROSS AS THE SIGN OF YOUR GRACE, WHERE
You offered Yourself not as King but as pawn
You switched all the letters of law in our case
OH, CHRIST TOOK SUCH GREAT LOSS FOR I SAY WE WERE GONE!

[CROSSOVER]

[REASSEMBLY #2:]

CURSED SIN GOES TOO FAR AND SO CHRIST'S AUGUST JOY, THE
Brave bearing of sorrow, was taking our place
Proud emblem of freedom is what we employ
SO THAT "CROSS-OUT" INDEED JUST HAS SIGNS OF YOUR GRACE!

[X-IT:]

Speak out the place … down at the cross!
Say to their face … tell 'em who's Boss!
Fear not your fate … Christ is His name!
'X' out the date … CHRISTmas reclaim!

For further reflection:
Mark 4:22; Luke 9:26; Acts 4:12; 1 Cor 1:18, 2:7; Gal 6:14

EIGHT LIVES DOWN

(Note: that super-eminent – though "least" – apostle seemed to have as many lives as a cat, per 2 Cor 11:25 for the first eight, but the ninth one not listed was the true keeper. So, let the stanza lines begin with eight "cat" words, leaving one you'll find elsewhere).

Cater-corner to some beastly fates
Caterwauling's out so save the wails
Categorical the dire straits
Catatonic looking dead as nails

Octuple's not the magic sum that rates
You can't rely on loopy crazy eights

Thrice beaten down where consciousness would slip
Once stoned and falling down (not getting high)
Thrice under water on a sinking ship
Once twenty-foured just watching waves go by
Not counting stripes that reached one-ninety-five
Each catastrophic, counted blow by blow
That cat's a phoenix from the ash alive
Still standing, eight lives down … and one to go

Catacombing caves in which to hide
Catapulted up when peril prods
Cataracts of danger's swelling tide
Catalyst for beating all the odds

Octuple's not the magic sum that rates
You can't rely on loopy crazy eights

Thrice beaten down where consciousness would slip

Once stoned and falling down (not getting high)
Thrice under water on a sinking ship
Once twenty-foured just watching waves go by
Not counting stripes that reached one-ninety-five
Each catastrophic, counted blow by blow
That cat's a phoenix from the ash alive
Still standing, eight lives down … and one to go

Those lives are water under bridges down
Still "feline fine" not wet or doomed to drown

When onslaughts all converge to challenge grace
And sweep on through to capture every pawn
The back-up plan will need to be in place
When life's not worth the skin it's printed on
You'll want to have the one marked number nine
It's always on reserve when stock gets low
So glad you'll be to see it next in line
When leaving here you'll need … that one to go

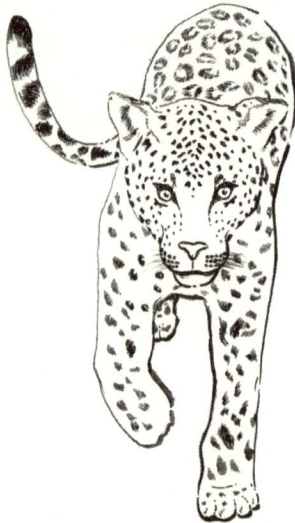

For further reflection:
Luke 9:23-24, 21:16-19; Acts 15:25-26; 2 Cor 11:23-27

WELL, I NEVER … !

So would you carry karaoke if your bucket dropped the tune? ….

I'd never bear a baritone if all his singing's just a croon
I'd never buy a biosphere without the shiny silver moon
I'd never sell a celebration if it ended way too soon
I'd never test a testament that came direct from God triune

I'd never top a topographic map with peaks far out of reach
I'd never know a Noah's ark if someone said it's at the beach
I'd never met a metaphysics ed who wasn't there to teach
I'd never fund a fundamentalist who didn't want to preach

But I will ever have to sever
Ties with those who won't say never
Few things here are sure forever
Missed by many counted clever

I'm sure I'll get a getaway that's upward bound at life's demise
I know I'm headed for the skies
I won't despise
That swell endeavor
I'm sure I'll dye a diadem to crown my Lord in holy hues
I know He's fully paid my dues
So don't accuse
With "Well, I never … !"

I'd never dare a derelict to come at me and pick a fight
I'd never chair a cherubim convention if it went all night
I'd never pick a Piccadilly if the circus traffic's tight
I'd never deck a Decalogue if all the laws were etched in right

I'd never dill a dilettante with pickle juice to crease his face
I'd never kill a kilowatt of energy that fuels my race
I'd never booed a Buddha head because its legs were out of place
I'd never rued a rudiment of doctrines showing saving grace

But I will ever have to sever
Ties with those who won't say never
Few things here are sure forever
Missed by many counted clever

I'm sure I'll get a getaway that's upward bound at life's demise
I know I'm headed for the skies
I won't despise
That swell endeavor
I'm sure I'll dye a diadem to crown my Lord in holy hues
I know He's fully paid my dues
So don't accuse
With "Well, I never … !"

You'd maybe press a precedent but keep in mind it's all or none
You'd maybe pen a penitent but always free him in the Son

For further reflection:
Matt 17:20; Mark 10:27; 2 Cor 1:17-20

NINE IN TEN AGREE

(Note the stanza rhyming pattern here – omnisyllabic. Okay, so I made that word up. Nevertheless, in each stanza, the first four lines rhyme with the second four lines, but not just from the last accented syllable forward. *All* the syllables rhyme in respective order. Yes, you may try this at home, but understand it will be at your own risk.)

Survey's in
Consensus in the data
Resting on efficient tool
It's not reflecting gratitude
Purvey sin?
Contentious in the beta
Testing on deficient pool
Fits lot rejecting attitude

If ten were cured, what's with the nine?
Perhaps the lone one's more than fine

Statistics always fail to show
The truth that few will ever know
You can't rely on its decree
Although refined to nth degree
And finding nine in ten agree

Lepers mum
Suggestion: try delaying
Turning, dare to mind the One
Yet sending healed to priest who there
Peppers some
Smug question: why be staying?
Learning where to find the Son

Met mending steeled who ceased to care

If ten were cured, what's with the nine?
Perhaps the lone one's more than fine

Statistics always fail to show
The truth that few will ever know
You can't rely on its decree
Although refined to nth degree
And finding nine in ten agree

Majority will never prove
His goodness, if so quick to move

Hey, so it's been really fun
But I'll see ya, gotta run

For further reflection:
Gen 18:23-32; Lev 13:45-46; Luke 17:12-19

UNSALTY SALT

When uncolored rainbows arch their bands across the sky
When uncloudy downpours leave the sidewalks dusty dry
When unbounded limits bring your planning to a halt
Then perhaps you'll season entrées with unsalty salt
When uncounted tallies yield results that don't repeat
When uncluttered messes make a massive chaos neat
When unquaking tremors make you wonder what's at fault
Then you'll sprinkle icy walkways with unsalty salt

Properties depend on what the substance really is
Not like calling soda water when it's lost its fizz

If you could become the very thing that you are not
That which cannot perish would be liable to rot
If the sum of parts can add up to a new gestalt
Then repentant tears you shed contain unsalty salt

When unrivaled equals must decide which one is best
When unbeaten losers learn of scores they can't contest
When undaunted cowards fight unfavored crony gangs
Then unsalty salt gets rubbed on aging meat that hangs
When unscented perfumes bring an odor-causing sneeze
When unwedded spouses pout each time that one agrees
When unharmful poisons make the perfect gourmet dish
Then unsalty salt in seas sustains the briny fish

Properties depend on what the substance really is
Not like calling soda water when it's lost its fizz

If you could become the very thing that you are not
That which cannot perish would be liable to rot

If the sum of parts can add up to a new gestalt
Then repentant tears you shed contain unsalty salt

If by any other name the rose is not a rose
Then it's really something else and all the sweetness goes
If the salt's become unsalty losing all its taste
Then it needs another name to show that it's a waste

When unheated Hades warms the cockles of your heart
When unhallowed heaven bids its saintly to depart
When unrighteous justice and unsparing mercy clash
Then you'll tromp unsalty salt just like compacted trash

For further reflection:
2 Kings 2:19-22; Job 6:6; Matt 5:13; Mark 9:50; Luke 14:34-35; Col 4:6;
Jas 3:11-12

POETIC MERCY

Sometimes sentences laconic
Spell out who must pay long dues
Inmates' cries are not symphonic
When endangered wails are blues
Still they chirp like jailhouse crickets
Humming bars that fix their homes
Lyric meter maids with tickets
Write up racecar palindromes

Isn't it just like His person?
Having left a prequel demo
So that when the tempos worsen
Signatures still mark His M.O.
Maybe love seemed in abeyance
As the sins just kept on growing
Strange, but law was made conveyance
That's poetic mercy showing

Dagwood hoagies (thin like Blondie?)
Light up every witty sconce
Some responder asks (re: spondee)
An' a pest can plague response
But he knows that brutal fact'll
Bode his death or even worse
When he tries to tear a dactyl
Bringing hex-ametric curse

Isn't it just like His person?
Having left a prequel demo
So that when the tempos worsen
Signatures still mark His M.O.

Maybe love seemed in abeyance
As the sins just kept on growing
Strange, but law was made conveyance
That's poetic mercy showing

Just as justice just is still
"A-verse" to strict iambic lines
Mercy's murmured trochees will
"Re-verse" crescendos' steep declines

Hard-core poets soften rhyming
But His rules won't be diminished
Just like punch lines' perfect timing
This must stop before it's ….

For further reflection:
Acts 17:28; Eph 2:10 (Greek: "poiema"); Jas 2:13; 1 Pet 2:10

Chapter 14

It's Really All About Him

The Lion's Share
For the God Who has Everything
Satellites Revolving Credit
At Least He's in a Better Place

THE LION'S SHARE

A fragment piece … that's all I seem to be
A shard, a scrap, a speck
A grain, a spot, a fleck
Not worth the time it takes to measure me

Yet by some grand contortion
I've bagged this huge proportion
I'm getting more than what I'd ever dreamed I'd get to see

The Pride of Judah's what's in store
I've got a mind to roar
The likes of my inheritance, to claim it who would dare?
For one who's no apostle
My take is so colossal
So see, I've made out big because I've snagged the Lion's share

Gigantic piece … that's what He is to me
Enormous, massive, great
Gargantuan, full plate
Beyond the scope of mere immensity

Yet by some grand contortion
He's got this tiny portion
He's getting less than heaven's best unaided eyes can see

This whelp He's called His claim to fame
He's given me His name
I'm not so much but when we're joined we make up quite a pair
His den is my apartment
My remake His department
So see, He'll trot me out with pride all tagged the Lion's share

I've got the Lion's share! … He's got the Lion's share!
He'd have me be aware: I AM the Lion's share!

So in the main He's set to gain this cub
To Him, affront, this puny runt to snub
His published will has got some special claws
The reading of it tends to give one paws

For further reflection:
Gen 49:9; Num 18:20; Psa 16:5, 28:9, 73:26, 106:5; Eph 1:14; Col 1:12;
Rev 5:5

FOR THE GOD WHO HAS EVERYTHING

The candles as votives looked nice
Plus flowers arranged like a heart
By choosing this kind of device
You're giving Him back His own art
He handles your motives just fine
Ignoring small points of finesse
Like scribblings young children design
It's love that He sees in the mess

His treasuries there are all full
Yet something's deficient – more thrones for His rule

So you're shopping for something to buy
And finding the merchandise stale
Remember His storehouse on high
Consider what gift would avail
Just think how few hearts fill His racks
He's yearning to build higher stacks
If you're looking for anything
God, who has everything,
Wants that one thing He still lacks

If silver and gold were too rare
He'd whip up a batch of His own
Of gem stones He's got His fair share
His cattle are also home grown
It's not that He has any need
Creation came late in His plan
One shortage could cause Him to bleed
To get what He's missing from man

His treasuries there are all full
Yet something's deficient – more thrones for His rule

So you're shopping for something to buy
And finding the merchandise stale
Remember His storehouse on high
Consider what gift would avail
Just think how few hearts fill His racks
He's yearning to build higher stacks
If you're looking for anything
God, who has everything,
Wants that one thing He still lacks

One stockpile's not groaning from weight
Just add your own soul there before it's too late

Just think how few hearts fill His racks
He's yearning to build higher stacks
There's a vast empty region though
Mansions are legion so
Now He's just looking for shacks

For further reflection:
Job 35:7, 41:11; Psa 50:10; Mark 12:41-44; Luke 21:5-6; John 14:2;
2 Cor 11:2

SATELLITES REVOLVING CREDIT

They're hurtling fast in outer space
But keep their center well in sight
Momentum helps maintain their pace
Rotation's bringing all to light
Trajectories are mapped with skill
So fellow travelers don't collide
And only those remaining still
Get back sides frozen, front sides fried

The closer worlds absorb for warming
Energy from solar rays
When comet clusters come in swarming
All positions stay in phase
When moons eclipse their star they dread it
Atmospheres cannot be mixed
Those satellites revolving credit
Suns that keep their orbits fixed

All drawn by gravitation's force
That won't let any globes escape
They exercise repeating course
So arcs of planets stay in shape
Unlike some pinball asteroid
That bounces off a neighbor rock
Deflected paths a trapezoid
Where rocket ships can never dock

The closer worlds absorb for warming
Energy from solar rays
When comet clusters come in swarming
All positions stay in phase

When moons eclipse their star they dread it
Atmospheres cannot be mixed
Those satellites revolving credit
Suns that keep their orbits fixed

The one that holds them all together
Gently tugs those far and near
Protected by an unseen tether
Left to run within their sphere

They've always had the heat they've needed
Never have they lacked a watt
It's just the clouds that have impeded
Beaming shafts that make them hot
Fierce radiation's not dissolving
Balls of earth that know their place
The credit's good for those revolving
Satellites reflecting grace

For further reflection:
Exo 34:29-35; John 1:4-9, 3:19-21, 5:35, 8:12; 1 Cor 15:40-41;
2 Cor 3:7-18; 1 John 1:5-7

AT LEAST HE'S IN A BETTER PLACE

The persecutors turned and smirked
As mourners watched His slumping face
So snide the cynic's phrasing worked:
"At least He's in a better place"

His vantage point is in a land
Where flesh and blood cannot erase
A single word of His command
At least He's in a better place

From heaven He will make our case
So much by far the better place

No longer bound by skin and bone
Though here of Him we find no trace
He's left His Spirit for His own
While reigning from a better place

We envy that disciple clan
Or children wrapped in His embrace
But now on high He sees each man
At least He's in a better place

No thrones down here a worthy seat
For throngs to worship at the base
This earth's a stool for sacred feet
At least He's in a better place

From heaven He will make our case
So much by far the better place

No longer bound by skin and bone
Though here of Him we find no trace
He's left His Spirit for His own
While reigning from a better place

We're not abandoned by our Spouse
He's gone away by pull of grace
Preparing there a finer house
We'll meet Him in that better place

For further reflection:
Matt 24:35, 27:39-43; Mark 9:36; John 14:2-3, 16:7; Acts 7:49;
1 John 2:1

Chapter 15

Reflections and Refractions

Time Once Was
Face Prints
Evil Ever Gently Comes
Rough the Winds
Turned to Snow

L. Richard De Prisco

TIME ONCE WAS

Time once was …
The days all dragged themselves along
And lingered on and on so long
Those days are gone
In youth it seemed so endless then
And I can still remember when
Clocks slowed at dawn
Time once was …

Time once was a long way back
From retrospect it had a knack
For standing still
Time once was a quick look to
A speedy end for days too few
But end it will

Time once was …
The days kept racing toward the eve
They kissed but never paused to cleave
Those days flew past
The speed just made their worth inflate
I rued the ratchet of each date
They went so fast
Time once was …

Time once was a long way back
From retrospect it had a knack
For standing still
Time once was a quick look to
A speedy end for days too few
But end it will

Time once was …
The measure of a cruel march
Until I passed on through the arch
That froze time there
And from its chains I'm thence set free
For in that place I'll always be
No longer where
… Time once was

For further reflection:
Psa 90:12; Eccl 3:11; Rom 13:11; 2 Pet 3:3-4, 8-12; Rev 1:3

FACE PRINTS

The signs are there for all to see
The handiwork that signs His name
On canvas where His artistry
Displays and spreads abroad His fame
The genius of that brilliant craft
So stunning for a single draft

See sky, see ground
Then pan creation all around
His footprints mark the dale and mound
And speak great volumes without sound
Watch in, watch out
The evidence erases doubt
His fingerprints still in the grout
That joins mosaic worlds about
But space remains where there's a hole
The empty depths where devils troll
A spot untouched that can't extol
Until His face prints stamp the soul

The image of divine we are
The countenance of God in flesh
That visage our reflections mar
A portrait sketch that cannot mesh
With holy outline not contained
In beauty here by sin profaned

Look left, look right
Observe the shapes in dimmest light
And blemishes that soon take flight
When Son-ray shafts invade the night

Gaze front, gaze back
Then let the likeness fill the crack
By tracing etchings where they lack
The figures formed in heaven's track
With all His face prints stenciled deep
In bold relief the contours leap
So clouded worldly ink won't seep
Into His face prints saints all keep

For further reflection:
Gen 1:27; Psa 19:1-6; Rom 1:19-21, 2 Cor 3:18, 4:6

EVIL EVER GENTLY COMES

The heart's the target, reddish-centered eye of bull
That's minded by that castle guard, the wary mind
So bowstrings send the arrows there, it has the pull
To sway the royal edict source those tips will find
They're sent like cherubs' loving darts
In cushy thoughts some point imparts
Its payload, penetration never causing smarts

A veil descends and cloaks the mask
To fool the ones who never ask

If frontal sallies were the surest way to strike
Attacks would need no cover in a harsh assault
Forensic evidence says give them what they like
Indulgence then extorts the claim it's not their fault
It mutes the brash disturbing drums
Enchanting with the sweetest hums
And hides the way that evil ever gently comes

To warm the faces where some cooler heads prevail
Come thawing rays through armor chinks exposing skin
It's common sense that ports of flesh would prove so frail
Enticing weakened reason into giving in
Decisions then are justified
By luxuries that worm inside
And take command of choices when discernment's died

A veil descends and cloaks the mask
To fool the ones who never ask

If frontal sallies were the surest way to strike

Attacks would need no cover in a harsh assault
Forensic evidence says give them what they like
Indulgence then extorts the claim it's not their fault
It mutes the brash disturbing drums
Enchanting with the sweetest hums
And hides the way that evil ever gently comes

Angelic tugs are often rough
While Satan's satins never scuff

The body politic will lobby varlet lies
To sway the seat of government that rules the soul
Revealed by hints of glints that flash from scarlet eyes
That importune with subtle lures but won't cajole
Arrangements never shout with mums
As prey are drawn with trails of crumbs
It's just the way that evil ever gently comes

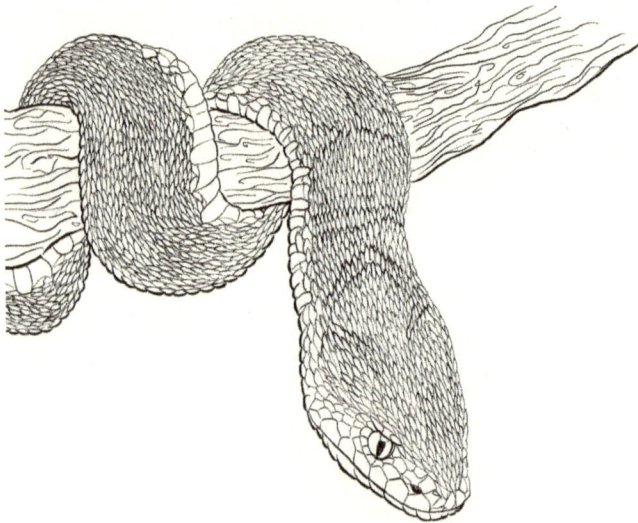

For further reflection:
Gen 3:1; Jer 17:9; Rom 6:19, 7:15-23, 8:5-8, 13:14; 2 Cor 11:14;
Gal 5:13

ROUGH THE WINDS

O gentle would the breezes be
In soft caress of rippled greens
They faintly nudge the sapling tree
But hazing not bucolic scenes
That world retains each fine-set edge
Where naught disturbs the fragile mounds
As whispers play the brittle sedge
To quiet creeks with soothing sounds

Yet harsh the paths that slice the vale
Retain their brusque and rigid spines
That never feel eroding gale
Or know the seas' corrosive brines
Untempered by insistent gusts
Some sheltered trail fierce squalls disdains
Untaught by blasts and scouring thrusts
That rough the winds make smooth the plains

Unetched the templates of that dell
Would scorn the scalpels of the sky
Where buffets build and greatly swell
To polish clear the stale and dry
Abrasive must those currents be
To wear encrusted, jagged down
And sweep away the shattered scree
Relaxing pastures' furrowed frown

Yet harsh the paths that slice the vale
Retain their brusque and rigid spines
That never feel eroding gale
Or know the seas' corrosive brines

Untempered by insistent gusts
Some sheltered trail fierce squalls disdains
Untaught by blasts and scouring thrusts
That rough the winds make smooth the plains

The mercy that was longed for most
Went undiscerned by raw-rubbed lands
Denuded by a howling host
Of chiseling chafes from skillful hands

The glossy surface carved from coarse
Invited bristling brush of air
That left no scars from callous force
Which clothed the heights at first made bare
The stagnant heavens proved more cruel
Than bursts that blistered fields of grain
The kindest was the sharpest tool
As rough the winds made clearly plain

For further reflection:
Job 37:21; Psa 104:4; Isa 21:1, 41:16; Jer 4:11-12; Zech 9:14; Luke 8:25;
Heb 1:7

TURNED TO SNOW

The downpour's been abated
It's all gently floating downward now
But I find I'm floating up somehow ....

Mud streaks wide across the lines
The ceaseless dripping constantly erodes the brain
Seamless sky has come undone
No one sees you chasing after
Finds you running down the drain

Atmosphere goes quiet
Darker now but luminescence rises from a field of light
As the fear flows by it
Let your face burn cold and ruddy
Funny how the red makes white
Pause a little even though you've turned to go
It looks as if it's turned to snow

Dreary's draped in muffling gauze
It's covered in acoustic garment muting sound
Blanching mottled rutted path
Someone sees you stifle laughter
Finds you running spritely gowned

Atmosphere goes quiet
Darker now but luminescence rises from a field of light
As the fear flows by it
Let your face burn cold and ruddy
Funny how the red makes white
Pause a little even though you've turned to go
It looks as if it's turned to snow

A cooling breeze is all it takes
Then breaks the ice with softer flakes

The downpour's been abated
It's all gently floating downward now
But I find I'm floating up somehow ….

For further reflection:
Psa 51:7; Isa 1:18, 55:10-11, Matt 8:24-27; Rev 19:8, 13-14

Chapter 16

After Affects (… All)

Jordan Rising
Outside the Box
Tomorrow's Just the History You Haven't Seen
Overtake the Undertaker
Kindergarter Snakes

L. Richard De Prisco

JORDAN RISING

He asked the crowd if there were any takers
River swells were high that day
I hesitated; were these big deal breakers?
Gamely, though, I felt the spray
I sensed refreshment from those cleansing billows
Coming up as from the dead
But no one there was selling any pillows
Places there to lay my head

Initial plunge, symbolic resting – pre-exam, not final testing
That will come … when Jordan's cresting

It brings on morbid terrors paralyzing
'Til its waters chill no more
Relieved I see it's just the Jordan rising
Comforts wash upon that shore
Next rendezvous' more bracing call for sinking
Bars ennui from tidal bore
I won't be sipping then but deeply drinking
End of battles, end of war

Those rivulets were streams of mercy running
Coming surge brings fear, unseen
Approaching closer opens views more stunning
Other coast is clear, serene
That last descent just seems intimidating
Will tsunamis froth and burst?
Pulled on from wading, revelation waiting,
I need full immersion first

Initial plunge, symbolic resting – pre-exam, not final testing

That will come ... when Jordan's cresting

It brings on morbid terrors paralyzing
'Til its waters chill no more
Relieved I see it's just the Jordan rising
Comforts wash upon that shore
Next rendezvous' more bracing call for sinking
Bars ennui from tidal bore
I won't be sipping then but deeply drinking
End of battles, end of war

The gentle currents mean no flood is brinking
There's no need to bar the door

And though it seems that it's my strength it's sapping
Lay me down, O soul, you'll keep
Be calmed to hear those peaceful ripples lapping
Lullabies to usher sleep

For further reflection:
Num 32:5, 32; 1 Chron 12:15; Job 40:23; Mark 10:38-39; Luke 12:50;
John 3:26; 1 Cor 15:26

OUTSIDE THE BOX

Some tunnel vision's fixed my gaze
Periphery's not what I see
With two-eyed focus right in phase
Wide angle never works for me

I must consider broader finds
Least, so I'm told by "open" minds

My skull is thick but opportunity still knocks
No-brainer head with feet and hands tied up in bonds and stocks
I concentrate but all I seem to build are mental blocks
I'm scolded once again to stop and think
Outside the box

But Someone set His face like flint
Not veering from prophetic script
For holding fast He did a stint
Three days and nights confined to crypt

I must consider broader finds
Least, so I'm told by "open" minds

My skull is thick but opportunity still knocks
No-brainer head with feet and hands tied up in bonds and stocks
I concentrate but all I seem to build are mental blocks
I'm scolded once again to stop and think
Outside the box

Expand your "out"-look experts say
Perspective's stuck on narrow way
But fish-eye view came into play

L. Richard De Prisco

When Angler caught my eye today

I'm not all there the day the mourners watch my casket sink
With brassy locks
It will be better then for me when I can clearly think
Outside the box

For further reflection:
Isa 50:7; Matt 7:13-14; Luke 9:51; 1 Cor 2:2; 2 Cor 6:7

TOMORROW'S JUST THE HISTORY
YOU HAVEN'T SEEN

Well that's a wrap
This film's all done
Those pieces on the floor will not get spun
No edits here
It's cut and print
The scenes are sealed, no trailer, not a hint

But rest assured
The good Director says you have endured

There's purpose for a hidden plot
This scripted veil
No preview seat, your bidden spot
Could here avail
To borrow from the mystery
Your test to screen
Tomorrow's just the history
You haven't seen

A storied life
Is what you'll live
Of future turns you can't be positive
The only way
You'd get it right
Is by a faith that's fully stripped of sight

But rest assured
The good Director says you have endured

There's purpose for a hidden plot

L. Richard De Prisco

This scripted veil
No preview seat, your bidden spot
Could here avail
To borrow from the mystery
Your test to screen
Tomorrow's just the history
You haven't seen

How did you do?
Results are in but can't be shown to you

So when they say, "You're history"
Don't stall your drive
Tomorrow won't stay mystery
You'll watch it live

For further reflection:
Deut 32:29; Eccl 3:11; Jer 29:11; Matt 6:34; 1 Tim 6:19; Jas 4:13-15

OVERTAKE THE UNDERTAKER

The race is on
The bulk of me is up for grabs
Who will get behind, most quarters,
Long before they pour the slabs?
Well, less is morgue
What's left of me in there's but dust
Booby prize but not the booty
When below in peace I rust

When the mausoleum's calling
Know that there I won't be stalling

Two are vying for remains
The day I thicken up the plot
One receives but One retains
The best not planted in that spot
Shining eyes, the one's no waker
He embalms but You're my Maker
Overtake the undertaker

He's catching on
Of corpse he knows the final score!
Falling back from leading early
Loser closes coffin door
I'm all caught up
So all they've done is hide the worst
Let your rector drag his service
Resurrector gets me first

When the mausoleum's calling
Know that there I won't be stalling

Two are vying for remains
The day I thicken up the plot
One receives but One retains
The best not planted in that spot
Shining eyes, the one's no waker
He embalms but You're my Maker
Overtake the undertaker

Advantage goes to One inside
He'd trounce the other if I died

Give his confidence a shaker
Rush ahead like record-breaker
Beat that slacker undertaker

For further reflection:
Luke 9:59-60, 12:4; 1 Cor 6:19, 15:35-50; 2 Cor 5:8; Phil 3:21;
1 Thes 4:17, 5:23; Jude 1:9

KINDERGARTER SNAKES

(Based strictly on Isa 11:6-9 … with poetic lic. no. 10367428)

Nurs'ry rhymes with curs'ry, like the kind of glance you'll give
Elevated threat's removed so all your tykes will live
Wolves won't need sheep's clothing since there's nothing left to hide
Calves will graze with mondo feline vegans in the pride

Infants need no flutes, just hands, for cobras at their den
Toddlers shaking rattlers keep their finger counts at ten
Bears will walk the Street not needing bulls, but cows will do
Leopards nap with little kids (yeah, yours, I thought you knew?)

Just for now these troubling thoughts can give you creepy jitters
But in time you'll be relaxed with all those creeping critters

Arm nips bring no gasps when asps have clasps with toothless gums
Children learning math will hold sharp adders doing sums
Who is minding babes, beg pardon?
No foreboding setting hard in
Safety zone none marred or scarred in
Panic's gone, you won't be doing any double takes
Not a role deceivers starred in
(Serpent Satan: turn your card in!)
Winding up for kinder-guardin':
Just "new-fang'led" vipers and some kindergarter snakes

Heroes don't get named but goats might qualify as subs
Tigers get no mention but could join those billy clubs
Tots reach into shark-filled tanks but don't just pull back stubs
Youths can hug big anacondas, then give belly rubs

Just for now these troubling thoughts can give you creepy jitters
But in time you'll be relaxed with all those creeping critters
Arm nips bring no gasps when asps have clasps with toothless gums
Children learning math will hold sharp adders doing sums
Who is minding babes, beg pardon?
No foreboding setting hard in
Safety zone none marred or scarred in
Panic's gone, you won't be doing any double takes
Not a role deceivers starred in
(Serpent Satan: turn your card in!)
Winding up for kinder-guardin':
Just "new-fang'led" vipers and some kindergarter snakes

"Predator" is lingo that will someday be passé
Frolicking (not running scared) will have a new cachet
Guess that holy mountain's gonna really be a zoo
Midst the fauna in my snapshots … there will I see you?

For further reflection:
Job 5:22-23; Isa 11:6-9, 65:25; Ezek 34:25; Hos 2:18

L. Richard De Prisco

Alphabetical Index of Poems

Abyssal Warming 73
Acrophobic, Falling 109
Amen to That 85
Applecartwheels 33
As Much Eternity as Time Permits 39
At Least He's in a Better Place 181
Between the Lines 15
Bought the Farm 21
Broken Dishes 149
Called Every Name in the Book 129
Carpe Deum 145
Confessions of a Holy Man 141
Crawling Butterflies 107
Cross-Eyed Yes but Twenty-Twenty 17
Disappointment Book 65
Eight Lives Down 163
Evil Ever Gently Comes 189
Face Prints 187
For the God Who has Everything 177
Genius with Three Wishes 135
Give It One More Shot 83
Healing Lame Excuses 151
He's Better Off Without Ur 51
He Thought, Therefore I Am 125
Hindsight Early on Foreseen 37
Holiday from Heresies 55
Homesick for a Place I've Never Seen 47
If the Sky's the Limit 53
If You Can? 103
It's Out of My Hands 19
Jerusalem Will Wait 59
Jordan Rising 197

Just Outside the Universe 43
Killing Time 67
Kindergarter Snakes 205
Lady of the Golden Streets 139
Leave the Old Man There to Rot 121
Levi's Genes 153
Like CPR for Corpses 157
Male Pattern Boldness 113
Mighty Servant Girl 117
Never Wasn't Soon Enough 29
Nine in Ten Agree 167
Nope, Just Can't, Sir 115
One Sky's Falling at a Time 105
One Thing Left They Cannot Do 57
Orthodox Orthotics 155
Outside the Box 199
Overtake the Undertaker 203
Palm Springs 23
Poetic Mercy 171
Postcard from the Netherlands 81
Primer for the Proper 79
Rough the Winds 191
Satellites Revolving Credit 179
Scenic Underwear 45
Should've Seen it Coming Down 75
Soft Apocalypse 143
Syndromicity 41
That's Just Not My Gift 91
The Lion's Share 175
Then Be That Way 95
Time Once Was 185
Tomorrow's Just the History You Haven't Seen 201
Too Much More of You 31
Turned to Snow 193
Under the Rainbow 63

Undying Love's Own Dying Lover 27
Unsalty Salt 169
Velvet Ultimatum 131
Wags that Dog Your Tail 93
Warriors in Therapy 119
Well, I Never ... ! 165
Where Crazies Rule the Roost 97
Who's to Blame? 127
Wisdom for Dummies 137
Wolves' Clothing 101
X-Word Puzzle 161
Youtuberculosis 89
Zodiac for Second Birth 69

L. Richard De Prisco

Chronological Index of Scriptural References

Gen 1:27	Face Prints
Gen 3:1	Evil Ever Gently Comes
Gen 3:6	Should've Seen It Coming Down
Gen 4:5-7	Then Be That Way
Gen 4:8-9	Should've Seen It Coming Down
Gen 7:17-23	Should've Seen It Coming Down
Gen 9:12-17	Under the Rainbow
Gen 11:31	He's Better Off Without Ur
Gen 18:23-32	Nine in Ten Agree
Gen 19:24-26	Should've Seen It Coming Down
Gen 22:14	Called Every Name in the Book
Gen 40:20-22	Should've Seen It Coming Down
Gen 49:9	The Lion's Share
Exo 14:5-9	Should've Seen It Coming Down
Exo 14:23-28	Should've Seen It Coming Down
Exo 15:26	Called Every Name in the Book
Exo 17:15	Called Every Name in the Book
Exo 20:26	Scenic Underwear
Exo 28:42-43	Scenic Underwear
Exo 34:6-7	Velvet Ultimatum
Exo 34:29-35	Satellites Revolving Credit
Lev 10:1-2	Should've Seen It Coming Down
Lev 13:45-46	Nine in Ten Agree
Lev 16:4	Scenic Underwear
Num 12:1-10	Should've Seen It Coming Down
Num 16:31-33	Should've Seen It Coming Down
Num 18:20	The Lion's Share
Num 32:5	Jordan Rising
Num 32:32	Jordan Rising
Deut 2:10	Should've Seen It Coming Down
Deut 5:32-33	Orthodox Orthotics

Deut 10:14	If the Sky's the Limit
Deut 29:22-28	Give It One More Shot
Deut 32:29	Tomorrow's Just the History You Haven't Seen
Deut 33:27	Acrophobic, Falling
Josh 1:6-9	Warriors in Therapy
Josh 6:1	Should've Seen It Coming Down
Josh 6:20	Should've Seen It Coming Down
Josh 7:20-26	Should've Seen It Coming Down
Josh 10:11	Should've Seen It Coming Down
Judg 1:4-7	Should've Seen It Coming Down
Judg 3:15-22	Should've Seen It Coming Down
Judg 4:17-22	Should've Seen It Coming Down
Judg 6:24	Called Every Name in the Book
Judg 9:52-54	Should've Seen It Coming Down
Judg 16:25-30	Should've Seen It Coming Down
Ruth 1:21	Nope, Just Can't, Sir
Ruth 2:5-9	Bought the Farm
1 Sam 17:34-37	Mighty Servant Girl
1 Sam 17:43-51	Should've Seen It Coming Down
1 Sam 21:13	Where Crazies Rule the Roost
2 Sam 8:15	Where Crazies Rule the Roost
2 Sam 11:2-4	Should've Seen It Coming Down
2 Sam 11:13-18	Should've Seen It Coming Down
2 Sam 16:5-8	Should've Seen It Coming Down
2 Sam 18:9-15	Should've Seen It Coming Down
2 Sam 22:34	Acrophobic, Falling
1 Kings 2:42-46	Should've Seen It Coming Down
1 Kings 8:27	If the Sky's the Limit
1 Kings 19:9-14	Soft Apocalypse
2 Kings 2:19-22	Unsalty Salt
2 Kings 2:23-24	Male Pattern Boldness
1 Chron 12:15	Jordan Rising
1 Chron 15:25-29	Applecartwheels
2 Chron 6:18	Just Outside the Universe
2 Chron 16:12	Nope, Just Can't, Sir

2 Chron 30:8	If You Can?
2 Chron 36:11-21	Jerusalem Will Wait
Ezra 6:3-22	Jerusalem Will Wait
Neh 8:10-12	Holiday from Heresies
Neh 9:7	He's Better Off Without Ur
Esther 6:12	Should've Seen It Coming Down
Esther 7:6-10	Should've Seen It Coming Down
Esther 9:17-22	Holiday from Heresies
Job 5:22-23	Kindergarter Snakes
Job 6:6	Unsalty Salt
Job 7:2-4	Disappointment Book
Job 10:9	Broken Dishes
Job 12:7-10	He Thought, Therefore I Am
Job 17:2	Wags that Dog Your Tail
Job 23:14-17	Disappointment Book
Job 33:13	Who's to Blame?
Job 35:7	For the God Who Has Everything
Job 36:3	Who's to Blame?
Job 37:21	Rough the Winds
Job 40:23	Jordan Rising
Job 41:11	For the God Who Has Everything
Psa 16:5	The Lion's Share
Psa 17:8	Applecartwheels
Psa 19:1-6	Face Prints
Psa 22:5	Disappointment Book
Psa 22:14	Between the Lines
Psa 22:16	It's Out of My Hands
Psa 23:1	Called Every Name in the Book
Psa 28:9	The Lion's Share
Psa 40:5	He Thought, Therefore I Am
Psa 50:10	For the God Who Has Everything
Psa 51:7	Turned to Snow
Psa 55:4	Between the Lines
Psa 55:6	Crawling Butterflies
Psa 66:9	Acrophobic, Falling

Psa 73:26	The Lion's Share
Psa 89:32	Between the Lines
Psa 90:12	Time Once Was
Psa 92:5	He Thought, Therefore I Am
Psa 92:15	Who's to Blame?
Psa 103:12	Just Outside the Universe
Psa 103:15	As Much Eternity as Time Permits
Psa 104:4	Rough the Winds
Psa 105:41	Palm Springs
Psa 106:5	The Lion's Share
Psa 106:15	Nope, Just Can't, Sir
Psa 118:6	One Thing Left They Cannot Do
Psa 118:13	Acrophobic, Falling
Psa 139:14-17	He Thought, Therefore I Am
Psa 139:17-18	Too Much More of You
Prov 1:20-33	Lady of the Golden Streets
Prov 2:10-19	Lady of the Golden Streets
Prov 3:13-18	Lady of the Golden Streets
Prov 4:7	Wisdom for Dummies
Prov 8:1-9:6	Lady of the Golden Streets
Prov 8:5	Wisdom for Dummies
Prov 9:10	Wisdom for Dummies
Prov 10:19	Wisdom for Dummies
Prov 11:2	Wisdom for Dummies
Prov 11:22	Primer for the Proper
Prov 13:10	Wisdom for Dummies
Prov 15:33	Wisdom for Dummies
Prov 17:28	Wisdom for Dummies
Prov 18:14	Nope, Just Can't, Sir
Prov 23:16	Then Be That Way
Prov 29:8	Wags that Dog Your Tail
Eccl 3:1	Disappointment Book
Eccl 3:11	Time Once Was
Eccl 3:11	Tomorrow's Just the History You Haven't Seen
Eccl 12:1	As Much Eternity as Time Permits

Song 2:3	Applecartwheels
Isa 1:18	Turned to Snow
Isa 5:20-21	Syndromicity
Isa 10:16	Nope, Just Can't, Sir
Isa 11:6-9	Kindergarter Snakes
Isa 12:6	Called Every Name in the Book
Isa 21:1	Rough the Winds
Isa 40:13-14	Who's to Blame?
Isa 40:29-31	Crawling Butterflies
Isa 41:16	Rough the Winds
Isa 43:20	Palm Springs
Isa 45:9	Who's to Blame?
Isa 47:3	Scenic Underwear
Isa 49:16	It's Out of My Hands
Isa 49:16	Palm Springs
Isa 50:7	Outside the Box
Isa 53:11-12	Bought the Farm
Isa 55:6	Carpe Deum
Isa 55:8-9	Too Much More of You
Isa 55:10-11	Turned to Snow
Isa 65:25	Kindergarter Snakes
Jer 4:11-12	Rough the Winds
Jer 17:9	Evil Ever Gently Comes
Jer 17:9	Too Much More of You
Jer 23:6	Called Every Name in the Book
Jer 29:4-14	Jerusalem Will Wait
Jer 29:11	Tomorrow's Just the History You Haven't Seen
Jer 31:1-9	Jerusalem Will Wait
Jer 52:8-11	Should've Seen It Coming Down
Lam 1:15	Disappointment Book
Lam 3:39-40	Who's to Blame?
Lam 4:2	Broken Dishes
Ezek 34:4	Nope, Just Can't, Sir
Ezek 36:26	Like CPR for Corpses
Ezek 37:1-10	Like CPR for Corpses

Ezek 48:35	Called Every Name in the Book
Dan 2:30	Too Much More of You
Dan 5:2-6	Should've Seen It Coming Down
Dan 5:25-30	Should've Seen It Coming Down
Dan 6:4-24	Should've Seen It Coming Down
Dan 7:9-14	Male Pattern Boldness
Dan 9:16-19	Jerusalem Will Wait
Hos 2:18	Kindergarter Snakes
Jonah 1:17	Disappointment Book
Jonah 1:17	Should've Seen It Coming Down
Jonah 3:4-10	Should've Seen It Coming Down
Jonah 4:1	Should've Seen It Coming Down
Jonah 4:6-8	Disappointment Book
Hab 3:19	Acrophobic, Falling
Hag 1:6	Like CPR for Corpses
Zech 7:9-8:23	Jerusalem Will Wait
Zech 9:14	Rough the Winds
Matt 3:10	Give It One More Shot
Matt 4:1-2	Cross-Eyed Yes but Twenty-Twenty
Matt 4:5	Cross-Eyed Yes but Twenty-Twenty
Matt 5:10	Warriors in Therapy
Matt 5:13	Unsalty Salt
Matt 5:16	Scenic Underwear
Matt 6:9-10	Under the Rainbow
Matt 6:19-20	As Much Eternity as Time Permits
Matt 6:34	Tomorrow's Just the History You Haven't Seen
Matt 7:13-14	Outside the Box
Matt 7:15	Wolves' Clothing
Matt 7:19	Give It One More Shot
Matt 8:24-27	Turned to Snow
Matt 10:16	Wolves' Clothing
Matt 10:28	One Thing Left They Cannot Do
Matt 10:38	Warriors in Therapy
Matt 11:12	Carpe Deum
Matt 11:29-30	Undying Love's Own Dying Lover

Matt 12:38-41	Zodiac for Second Birth
Matt 13:15	Healing Lame Excuses
Matt 13:44	Bought the Farm
Matt 14:28-29	Mighty Servant Girl
Matt 15:25	Called Every Name in the Book
Matt 15:28	Genius With Three Wishes
Matt 16:1-3	Zodiac for Second Birth
Matt 16:1-4	Should've Seen It Coming Down
Matt 16:2-3	Hindsight Early on Foreseen
Matt 16:2-3	One Sky's Falling at a Time
Matt 16:21	Cross-Eyed Yes but Twenty-Twenty
Matt 16:21-22	Mighty Servant Girl
Matt 17:20	Well, I Never … !
Matt 20:1-16	Bought the Farm
Matt 20:30-34	Carpe Deum
Matt 21:5	Soft Apocalypse
Matt 21:19	Give It One More Shot
Matt 21:22	Genius With Three Wishes
Matt 21:33-43	Bought the Farm
Matt 21:44	Acrophobic, Falling
Matt 23:13-33	Amen to That
Matt 23:24	Wags that Dog Your Tail
Matt 23:25-28	Primer for the Proper
Matt 23:37	Male Pattern Boldness
Matt 24:29-31	One Sky's Falling at a Time
Matt 24:35	At Least He's in a Better Place
Matt 24:42-44	Hindsight Early on Foreseen
Matt 24:42-51	Killing Time
Matt 25:13	Hindsight Early on Foreseen
Matt 25:14-30	That's Just Not My Gift
Matt 25:31	Postcard from the Netherlands
Matt 25:41	Abyssal Warming
Matt 26:64	Cross-Eyed Yes but Twenty-Twenty
Matt 26:69-74	Mighty Servant Girl
Matt 27:3-5	Should've Seen It Coming Down

Matt 27:39-43	At Least He's in a Better Place
Mark 2:2-5	Carpe Deum
Mark 2:4	Healing Lame Excuses
Mark 2:17	Healing Lame Excuses
Mark 2:22	Applecartwheels
Mark 3:21	Where Crazies Rule the Roost
Mark 4:3-20	Bought the Farm
Mark 4:22	X-Word Puzzle
Mark 6:2	It's Out of My Hands
Mark 9:20-24	If You Can?
Mark 9:36	At Least He's in a Better Place
Mark 9:50	Unsalty Salt
Mark 10:27	Well, I Never … !
Mark 10:35-40	Genius With Three Wishes
Mark 10:38-39	Jordan Rising
Mark 11:24	Genius With Three Wishes
Mark 12:41-44	For the God Who Has Everything
Mark 13:20	Killing Time
Mark 13:28-29	Should've Seen It Coming Down
Mark 13:33-37	Killing Time
Mark 14:66-72	Wolves' Clothing
Mark 15:31-32	Male Pattern Boldness
Luke 1:18-22	Should've Seen It Coming Down
Luke 1:59-63	Should've Seen It Coming Down
Luke 1:64	Where Crazies Rule the Roost
Luke 6:41-42	Amen to That
Luke 8:25	Rough the Winds
Luke 8:42-48	Carpe Deum
Luke 8:43-44	Healing Lame Excuses
Luke 9:23	Leave the Old Man There to Rot
Luke 9:23-24	Eight Lives Down
Luke 9:26	X-Word Puzzle
Luke 9:51	Outside the Box
Luke 9:59-60	Overtake the Undertaker
Luke 11:53-54	Wags that Dog Your Tail

Luke 12:2-3	Youtuberculosis
Luke 12:4	Overtake the Undertaker
Luke 12:16-21	Bought the Farm
Luke 12:22-24	If You Can?
Luke 12:50	Jordan Rising
Luke 12:54-56	Hindsight Early on Foreseen
Luke 12:54-57	Should've Seen It Coming Down
Luke 13:6-9	Give It One More Shot
Luke 14:16-24	Healing Lame Excuses
Luke 14:34-35	Unsalty Salt
Luke 15:11-32	Bought the Farm
Luke 16:15	Syndromicity
Luke 16:19-31	Postcard from the Netherlands
Luke 16:22-25	Abyssal Warming
Luke 17:12-19	Nine in Ten Agree
Luke 19:2-9	Carpe Deum
Luke 19:11-27	Male Pattern Boldness
Luke 20:20	Wags that Dog Your Tail
Luke 20:26	Wags that Dog Your Tail
Luke 21:5-6	For the God Who Has Everything
Luke 21:14-15	Wisdom for Dummies
Luke 21:16-19	Eight Lives Down
Luke 21:34-36	Hindsight Early on Foreseen
Luke 22:1-23:46	Should've Seen It Coming Down
Luke 22:56-60	Mighty Servant Girl
Luke 24:50	It's Out of My Hands
John 1:4-9	Satellites Revolving Credit
John 3:19-21	Satellites Revolving Credit
John 3:26	Jordan Rising
John 4:13-14	Palm Springs
John 5:35	Satellites Revolving Credit
John 6:48-51	Undying Love's Own Dying Lover
John 7:24	Primer for the Proper
John 7:38	Palm Springs
John 7:38	Then Be That Way

John 8:12	Satellites Revolving Credit
John 8:23-24	Postcard from the Netherlands
John 9:1-3	Who's to Blame?
John 9:40-41	Too Much More of You
John 10:3-5	Never Wasn't Soon Enough
John 10:11-15	Wolves' Clothing
John 10:20	Where Crazies Rule the Roost
John 10:28-29	It's Out of My Hands
John 10:30	Cross-Eyed Yes but Twenty-Twenty
John 12:24	Bought the Farm
John 12:27	Cross-Eyed Yes but Twenty-Twenty
John 13:13	It's Out of My Hands
John 14:1-3	Under the Rainbow
John 14:2	For the God Who Has Everything
John 14:2-3	At Least He's in a Better Place
John 14:8-10	Cross-Eyed Yes but Twenty-Twenty
John 14:13-14	Under the Rainbow
John 14:21-23	Homesick for a Place I've Never Seen
John 15:7	Genius With Three Wishes
John 15:16	Never Wasn't Soon Enough
John 15:20	Warriors in Therapy
John 15:22	Healing Lame Excuses
John 16:7	At Least He's in a Better Place
John 16:13-15	Homesick for a Place I've Never Seen
John 17:24-26	Undying Love's Own Dying Lover
John 18:10	Mighty Servant Girl
John 20:22	Like CPR for Corpses
John 20:24-28	Then Be That Way
John 20:25	Palm Springs
John 20:25-28	It's Out of My Hands
John 20:28	Cross-Eyed Yes but Twenty-Twenty
John 20:29	Homesick for a Place I've Never Seen
Acts 1:9-11	If the Sky's the Limit
Acts 3:8	Applecartwheels
Acts 4:12	X-Word Puzzle

Acts 5:1-5	Then Be That Way
Acts 7:49	At Least He's in a Better Place
Acts 11:17	That's Just Not My Gift
Acts 15:25-26	Eight Lives Down
Acts 17:27	Carpe Deum
Acts 17:28	Poetic Mercy
Rom 1:19-21	Face Prints
Rom 1:19-22	He Thought, Therefore I Am
Rom 1:20	Healing Lame Excuses
Rom 2:1	Healing Lame Excuses
Rom 2:4-5	If You Can?
Rom 2:4-10	Velvet Ultimatum
Rom 3:25	Velvet Ultimatum
Rom 5:5	Disappointment Book
Rom 5:6	Never Wasn't Soon Enough
Rom 5:7-8	Like CPR for Corpses
Rom 6:3-11	Like CPR for Corpses
Rom 6:6-11	Leave the Old Man There to Rot
Rom 6:19	Evil Ever Gently Comes
Rom 7:15-23	Evil Ever Gently Comes
Rom 8:5-8	Evil Ever Gently Comes
Rom 8:10	Leave the Old Man There to Rot
Rom 8:35-39	One Thing Left They Cannot Do
Rom 9:19-21	Who's to Blame?
Rom 9:22	Velvet Ultimatum
Rom 9:22-23	Broken Dishes
Rom 9:22-23	Never Wasn't Soon Enough
Rom 9:33	Disappointment Book
Rom 10:8-10	Confessions of a Holy Man
Rom 10:15	Orthodox Orthotics
Rom 10:21	It's Out of My Hands
Rom 11:16	Confessions of a Holy Man
Rom 11:22	Velvet Ultimatum
Rom 11:29	That's Just Not My Gift
Rom 11:33	He Thought, Therefore I Am

Rom 11:33-34	Too Much More of You
Rom 12:2	Wolves' Clothing
Rom 12:6	That's Just Not My Gift
Rom 13:11	Time Once Was
Rom 13:14	Evil Ever Gently Comes
1 Cor 1:7	That's Just Not My Gift
1 Cor 1:18	X-Word Puzzle
1 Cor 1:18-29	Where Crazies Rule the Roost
1 Cor 1:22-25	Zodiac for Second Birth
1 Cor 2:2	Outside the Box
1 Cor 2:7	X-Word Puzzle
1 Cor 2:10-16	He Thought, Therefore I Am
1 Cor 3:1-4	Crawling Butterflies
1 Cor 3:17	Confessions of a Holy Man
1 Cor 3:17	One Thing Left They Cannot Do
1 Cor 4:9-10	Where Crazies Rule the Roost
1 Cor 4:11-13	Warriors in Therapy
1 Cor 4:16-5:4	As Much Eternity as Time Permits
1 Cor 6:19	Overtake the Undertaker
1 Cor 7:7	That's Just Not My Gift
1 Cor 10:13	One Sky's Falling at a Time
1 Cor 13:5	Undying Love's Own Dying Lover
1 Cor 13:6	Holiday from Heresies
1 Cor 13:7-8	Undying Love's Own Dying Lover
1 Cor 13:13	That's Just Not My Gift
1 Cor 14:1	That's Just Not My Gift
1 Cor 14:12	That's Just Not My Gift
1 Cor 14:25	Too Much More of You
1 Cor 15:26	Jordan Rising
1 Cor 15:35-50	Overtake the Undertaker
1 Cor 15:40-41	Satellites Revolving Credit
2 Cor 1:17-20	Well, I Never … !
2 Cor 3:7-18	Satellites Revolving Credit
2 Cor 3:18	Face Prints
2 Cor 4:2	Youtuberculosis

2 Cor 4:6	Face Prints
2 Cor 4:7	Broken Dishes
2 Cor 4:8-11	Warriors in Therapy
2 Cor 4:16	Scenic Underwear
2 Cor 5:2-4	Scenic Underwear
2 Cor 5:8	Overtake the Undertaker
2 Cor 6:7	Outside the Box
2 Cor 8:9	Never Wasn't Soon Enough
2 Cor 8:9	Undying Love's Own Dying Lover
2 Cor 10:1-2	Male Pattern Boldness
2 Cor 10:12	Syndromicity
2 Cor 11:1	Where Crazies Rule the Roost
2 Cor 11:2	For the God Who Has Everything
2 Cor 11:14	Evil Ever Gently Comes
2 Cor 11:17	Where Crazies Rule the Roost
2 Cor 11:21	Where Crazies Rule the Roost
2 Cor 11:23	Where Crazies Rule the Roost
2 Cor 11:23-27	Eight Lives Down
2 Cor 11:30	Where Crazies Rule the Roost
2 Cor 12:2	If the Sky's the Limit
2 Cor 12:6	Where Crazies Rule the Roost
2 Cor 12:7-9	Nope, Just Can't, Sir
2 Cor 12:11	Where Crazies Rule the Roost
Gal 2:11-14	Wolves' Clothing
Gal 2:20	Leave the Old Man There to Rot
Gal 4:4	Never Wasn't Soon Enough
Gal 5:13	Evil Ever Gently Comes
Gal 5:24	Leave the Old Man There to Rot
Gal 6:12	Warriors in Therapy
Gal 6:14	Leave the Old Man There to Rot
Gal 6:14	X-Word Puzzle
Gal 6:14	Zodiac for Second Birth
Eph 1:4	Confessions of a Holy Man
Eph 1:14	The Lion's Share
Eph 2:10 (Gk: poiema)	Poetic Mercy

Eph 2:13-16	Cross-Eyed Yes but Twenty-Twenty
Eph 2:21	Confessions of a Holy Man
Eph 3:16	Then Be That Way
Eph 4:7	That's Just Not My Gift
Eph 4:10	If the Sky's the Limit
Eph 4:22	Leave the Old Man There to Rot
Eph 5:15-16	Killing Time
Eph 5:27	Confessions of a Holy Man
Eph 6:10-17	Warriors in Therapy
Eph 6:15	Orthodox Orthotics
Phil 1:27-28	Zodiac for Second Birth
Phil 2:7	Never Wasn't Soon Enough
Phil 3:19	Youtuberculosis
Phil 3:21	Overtake the Undertaker
Phil 4:8	Holiday from Heresies
Phil 4:17	That's Just Not My Gift
Col 1:12	The Lion's Share
Col 1:22	Confessions of a Holy Man
Col 3:5-9	Leave the Old Man There to Rot
Col 4:5	Killing Time
Col 4:6	Unsalty Salt
1 Thes 2:7-8	Soft Apocalypse
1 Thes 4:17	Overtake the Undertaker
1 Thes 4:17	Where Crazies Rule the Roost
1 Thes 5:1-8	Hindsight Early on Foreseen
1 Thes 5:23	Overtake the Undertaker
2 Thes 3:11	Youtuberculosis
1 Tim 2:9-10	Primer for the Proper
1 Tim 4:14	That's Just Not My Gift
1 Tim 5:13	Youtuberculosis
1 Tim 6:3-5	Orthodox Orthotics
1 Tim 6:6	If You Can?
1 Tim 6:16	Just Outside the Universe
1 Tim 6:19	Tomorrow's Just the History You Haven't Seen
2 Tim 2:3	Warriors in Therapy

2 Tim 2:6	That's Just Not My Gift
2 Tim 2:20	Broken Dishes
2 Tim 3:2-5	Amen to That
2 Tim 3:12	Warriors in Therapy
2 Tim 4:3	Amen to That
2 Tim 4:3-4	Orthodox Orthotics
2 Tim 4:5-7	Warriors in Therapy
Heb 1:7	Rough the Winds
Heb 2:9-10	Between the Lines
Heb 5:12-6:2	Crawling Butterflies
Heb 6:7-8	Give It One More Shot
Heb 6:20	Levi's Genes
Heb 7:11-19	Levi's Genes
Heb 10:39	Warriors in Therapy
Heb 11:8-10	He's Better Off Without Ur
Heb 11:13-16	Homesick for a Place I've Never Seen
Heb 11:14-16	He's Better Off Without Ur
Heb 12:3	One Sky's Falling at a Time
Heb 12:3-13	Warriors in Therapy
Heb 13:6	One Thing Left They Cannot Do
Jas 1:5	Wisdom for Dummies
Jas 1:22	Amen to That
Jas 2:1-4	Primer for the Proper
Jas 2:13	Poetic Mercy
Jas 3:11-12	Unsalty Salt
Jas 4:3	Genius With Three Wishes
Jas 4:7	If You Can?
Jas 4:13-15	Tomorrow's Just the History You Haven't Seen
Jas 4:14	As Much Eternity as Time Permits
Jas 5:1-5	Primer for the Proper
1 Pet 1:8	Applecartwheels
1 Pet 1:14-15	Wolves' Clothing
1 Pet 2:9	Confessions of a Holy Man
1 Pet 2:9	Levi's Genes
1 Pet 2:10	Poetic Mercy

1 Pet 3:20	Velvet Ultimatum
1 Pet 4:10	That's Just Not My Gift
2 Pet 3:3	Wags that Dog Your Tail
2 Pet 3:3-4	Time Once Was
2 Pet 3:8-12	Time Once Was
2 Pet 3:9	Velvet Ultimatum
2 Pet 3:10-12	Abyssal Warming
2 Pet 3:15	Velvet Ultimatum
1 John 1:5-7	Satellites Revolving Credit
1 John 2:1	At Least He's in a Better Place
1 John 2:28	Warriors in Therapy
1 John 4:4	One Thing Left They Cannot Do
1 John 4:8	Undying Love's Own Dying Lover
1 John 4:16	Undying Love's Own Dying Lover
1 John 5:14-15	Genius With Three Wishes
Jude 1:9	Overtake the Undertaker
Jude 1:13	Youtuberculosis
Jude 1:18	Wags that Dog Your Tail
Rev 1:3	Time Once Was
Rev 3:18	Scenic Underwear
Rev 5:5	The Lion's Share
Rev 5:5	Zodiac for Second Birth
Rev 5:9-10	Levi's Genes
Rev 7:9-14	Scenic Underwear
Rev 8:1-4	Soft Apocalypse
Rev 11:6	One Sky's Falling at a Time
Rev 11:10-13	Holiday from Heresies
Rev 11:12	If the Sky's the Limit
Rev 15:1	Zodiac for Second Birth
Rev 16:8-9	Abyssal Warming
Rev 19:8	Turned to Snow
Rev 19:13-14	Turned to Snow
Rev 19:20	Should've Seen It Coming Down
Rev 20:1-4	Should've Seen It Coming Down
Rev 20:6	Levi's Genes

Rev 20:10-15	Should've Seen It Coming Down
Rev 20:11	Just Outside the Universe
Rev 21:1	Just Outside the Universe
Rev 21:2-21	Jerusalem Will Wait
Rev 21:8	Warriors in Therapy
Rev 22:14	Should've Seen It Coming Down

Richard De Prisco is available for speaking engagements and personal appearances. For more information contact:

L. Richard De Prisco
Advantage Books
P.O. Box 160847
Altamonte Springs, FL 32716

info@ advbooks.com

To purchase additional copies of this book or other books published by Advantage Books call our toll free order number at:
1-888-383-3110 (Book Orders Only)

or visit our bookstore website at:
www.advbookstore.com

*A*dvantage
BOOKS

Longwood, Florida, USA
"we bring dreams to life"™
www.advbooks.com

www.ingramcontent.com/pod-product-compliance
Lightning Source LLC
Chambersburg PA
CBHW020850090426
42736CB00008B/324